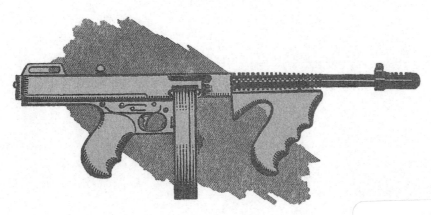

GREAT BRITAIN -

THE

TOMMY

GUN

STORY

Great Britain – The Tommy Gun Story

by

Tom Davis, Jr.

For Janet & Thomas
and
Auntie Lil -
who taught me writing a book is possible!

Acknowledgements

This story would not have been possible without the tenacious and informed research of Mr. James West. James visited the National Archives on numerous occasions on behalf of the author and provided the great majority of the documentation cited in this story. He tirelessly looked for every piece of paper that would help tell the story of the Tommy gun in Great Britain during World War II. He also spent a great deal of time teaching the author about the remarkable men involved with the procurement of the Thompson gun. Those that know James will recognize his vast knowledge of military history throughout the story. Without his continuing help, the author would have never understood the interaction of the people and acronyms cited in this story. The many tables featured toward the end of this book are the work of James. All accolades for this story belong to James; I accept complete responsibility for any gaffes that may appear.

My journey into writing stories about the Thompson submachine gun would never have started without the help of David Albert and Tracie Hill. Their assistance over the years has kept the research and writing fun. I also wish to thank Frank Iannamico for sharing information with me from his reference collection and never once asking what I was doing. And to Robert Segel, the Senior Editor at *Small Arms Review* magazine, who always makes my stories better. Their early guidance and assistance on previous stories made me comfortable taking on this project. May this work by James and me be something that makes all these accomplished writers proud.

I would also like to thank Michael Sigillito for teaching me the model 28 Navy was a solution to a non-existent problem! While researching old records for information on the Thompson is enjoyable, shooting the Thompson gun is much more fun. A little trigger time at the yearly Hill family All Thompson Show & Shoot provides the necessary encouragement to start and, more importantly, complete this type of undertaking. The many members of The American Thompson Association and the Thompson Collectors Association are simply the best.

The Internet can be a wonderful place. The Thompson submachine gun forum at www.MachineGunBoards.com is home to many a Thompson enthusiast. James and I first talked on that site. There is no ocean separating us in cyberspace.

As you turn the pages, you will note pictures of many items credited to different enthusiasts and collections around the world. It gives me great pleasure to include their names and honor their contributions. This book is the labors of many.

The time I spent writing this story was time I did not spend with my lovely wife Janet and wonderful son Thomas. While this time can never be replaced, their love and encouragement is always treasured. A man that has a loving family and good friends wants for nothing. I would be remiss not mentioning our new Lakeland terrier, Tango. He is such a joy - and is looking up at me right now wanting to go for a walk!

All will have been worthwhile if this story preserves the behind the scenes world of the heroes involved in the procurement of the Thompson gun for the British military. If not for their efforts, that terrible war may have been much longer.

T.K.D., Jr.
Union, Kentucky

Contents

Foreword

The Thompson Submachine Gun embodies perhaps the richest history of any of the world's firearms. It amazes me how its history is mentioned in everyday conversations, appears on television and in social media circles, and is known by almost anyone as the "Tommy Gun." It's somewhat of a pop culture icon, extending back almost a century.

Tom Davis and I shared various collector transactions in the early 2000's, and finally met at the Thompson Collector's Association Show and Shoot hosted by the Tracie Hill family in Ohio in 2005. When I moved from Texas to Ohio in 2006, with Tom living 45 minutes away in Kentucky, we began attending several shows together on a regular basis, including Knob Creek Machine Gun Shoots, Louisville Gun Shows, various NRA Conventions, annual meetings of The American Thompson Association and the Thompson Collectors Association, and the Ohio Gun Collectors Association. Tom also taught me skeet shooting, a sport for which he possesses exceptional skill. A thirst for Thompson history began, and continues to fuel our friendship.. Writing is an outlet for my Thompson passion, as well as for other firearms. My first article was published by Small Arms Review (SAR) in 2005, and I subsequently researched some Thompson articles that appeared in later issues. These articles intrigued Tom, and he began to research and write on various other Thompson subjects. He now has numerous well researched articles on the Thompson, also published by SAR. We both contributed to the 2009 Tracie Hill book, "The Ultimate Thompson Book," and continue to share our notes and new discoveries on the subject.

It's no revelation to even the most casual historian that Britain faced a battle for its survival in 1940. Short of arms, under nightly attack by the Luftwaffe, and fearing a potentially imminent invasion, the urgency drove decisions that quickly brought the Thompson across the Atlantic to shore up British defenses. The fall of France in June summoned an even grimmer outlook, and the floodgates of British efforts and resources came forth to save the country from German occupation. The Thompson Submachine Gun played a major role in protecting Britain and the Commonwealth nations throughout the war.

In this book, Tom presents detailed and annotated research of the acquisition of the Thompson Submachine Gun by the British through various government agencies, under two different U.S. acquisition policies, namely "Cash and Carry," and "Lend Lease." French, Swedish, and Canadian orders are also reviewed as they relate to British Thompson procurement. He puts to rest various speculations pervaded by the collector community to date, including the documented figures of Atlantic transportation losses, and the number of Colt Thompsons that saw British service. He also provides an excellent tutorial of marking differences between Colt, Savage, and Auto-Ordnance Bridgeport manufactured Thompsons, which is useful to collectors who may own, encounter, or just have a general interest in the subtle differences inherent to this classic firearm.

Because the history of the Thompson is so rich and long, with succession of the Thompson product extending from 1916 to present day, the areas for additional research that still exist remain abundant. I personally know that this book, a professionally published draft copy of which was first delivered to me in January 2014, will inspire me to reach further in my Thompson documentary efforts, as Tom has set a high bar with his work on this subject. He is always careful to research, analyze, and present findings in a manner that will stand the test of time, while enabling others to build on his work, should they so desire. His approach methodology is a trait of both his legal and law enforcement backgrounds. Tom also includes contributions of the Thompson collector community in the book, most notably the enablement of the work through the gathering and contextual efforts of James West in the U.K.

Britain and the U.S. owe much to John T. Thompson and the talented group of engineers and others who designed, built, and marketed the weapon bearing his name. The Thompson Submachine Gun served both countries exceptionally well, and is one of a select few small arms that arguably tipped the scales in favor of allied victory in two battle theatres. Tom's research of British Thompson history should become well received by readers among both nations, as well as other global firearm history enthusiasts.

David Albert
October 2014

Prologue

The Thompson submachine gun has been involved in many wars and causes since its introduction in 1921. The tremendous use and popularity of this first American submachine gun has resulted in hundreds of published stories and articles. While some are carefully researched and written, others report as fact much of the inaccurate folklore or pure fiction that has arisen with the use (and misuse) of this now iconic firearm. This story is about the adoption and procurement of the Thompson gun by the British armed forces during World War II - with an emphasis on procurement. It is based entirely on actual documentation, most of it taken directly from the preserved Ministry of Supply (MoS) records at the National Archives in London. Every aspect of this story is supported by a document written long ago, a recorded meeting and/or some other type of irrefutable proof. While the documentation is extensive, there is no claim the documentation is complete - or completely understandable. Discrepancies exist, primarily with the procurement numbers. Much of the verbiage, including the various date styles, different spellings, abbreviations and telegram grammar, is taken directly from the original documents. This story is written especially for those Thompson enthusiasts who want every detail of information, every single crumb - no matter how small - and may never be able to review the actual documentation.

Chapter One: The Procurement

Great Britain was one of the first governments offered a personal demonstration of the new Thompson gun. On June 30, 1921, General John T. Thompson and Auto-Ordnance Corporation (AOC) employee George E. Goll demonstrated this American invention to representatives of the British Royal Air Force, Admiralty, War Office, India Office, Australian Commonwealth and the Metropolitan Police at the Royal Small Arms Factory at Enfield. The report of the demonstration and subsequent tests of the Thompson gun seemed favorable - but no orders were forthcoming. The British were not alone in their decision not to purchase the Thompson gun; sales calls to other governments across the world met a similar fate. [1]

As the talk of war gripped Europe in the 1930s a series of Neutrality Acts were passed by the United States Congress to prevent intervention in the affairs of other countries. The memories of World War I were still fresh and many in the USA embraced a growing policy of isolationism. In September 1939, two historic events caused President Franklin D. Roosevelt to petition Congress for a change in the current Neutrality Act: Germany invaded Poland and France and Great Britain declared war on Germany. The Neutrality Act of 1939 (passed in November 1939), allowed for the purchase of munitions from the United States by warring or belligerent nations when paid for by cash, and carried away from American shores in non-US vessels. Ostensibly even-handed, the policy in practice favored Great Britain and France who were in a position to thwart Germany's access to the seas and exercise freedom of the seas themselves. Therefore, 'cash-and-carry' was born. The British Treasury soon realized that Britain's dollar reserves were all too small and wished to restrict dollar expenditures to only essential items.

A short step to 1940 finds Great Britain deep at war with a well-equipped Nazi Germany and in desperate need of military equipment. In an instant, the long ago military objections to weapons like the Thompson gun vanished. Matters would soon get worse with the evacuation of British forces at the French port of Dunkirk and the possible invasion of Britain by Germany. Regardless of how bad it may have been in Britain during the early days of the war, one thing remained constant – the bureaucracy of the British War Office in obtaining the necessary implements of war. This required paperwork and lots of it. While London was burning paperwork was flowing to bring this island Kingdom the required tools to win the war. To that end, we can be grateful that much of the paperwork survived these many years, carefully stored away at the National Archives. The key is being able to find it!

The War Office,
Whitehall,
S.W.1.

The First Order

On January 19, 1940, R.J. Sinclair, Director General of Army Requirements (D.G.A.R) at the War Office, penned a SECRET, and private letter to Lt. General Sir Maurice G. Taylor, Senior Military

---

[1] Tracie L. Hill, et. al., *The Ultimate Thompson Book* (Canada: Collector Grade Publications, 2009), 130-135

Advisor to the Minister of Supply, advising him that approval had been given at the War Office for the procurement of 750 Thompson guns and 3 million rounds of ammunition. [2] This order was a very noteworthy event in that Sinclair ended the letter with, "I thought that you might be interested to have the earliest possible intimation of this." At the time, there is no way Sinclair could have envisioned this letter would document the first of what would be many British orders for the Thompson submachine gun. A day earlier, a Cypher Telegram (Canada) from Colonel J.H.M. Greenly, Controller-General, British Supply Board (BSB) in Canada, to Engineer Vice Admiral Sir Harold Brown, Director General Munitions Production or D.G.M.P., Ministry of Supply (MoS), told of how 600 Thompson guns without compensators were presently available for purchase and cited future delivery schedules. The price was $175 per gun without compensator. A handwritten notation at the end of the telegram stated, "Compensators $25." [3] The British were in the market for an American gangster gun.

A SECRET Ministry of Supply (MoS) Memorandum No. 15/40 dated 24th January, 1940 set forth the official request from the War Office to obtain 750 Thompson guns at £37,500. Also included were an unspecified number of magazines at £19,500 and 3 million rounds of .45 caliber ammunition at £25,000 for a total purchase price of £82,000. [4] A memorandum dated January 26th from E.G. Compton, British Treasury, advised receipt of the above MoS Memorandum - "We are discussing this proposal with the War Office." [5] The British Treasury approved the purchase of £82,000 of Thompson guns, accessories and ammunition on January 31st with the expressed assurance from the MoS that any further quantities of ammunition would be produced in Great Britain. The Treasury wanted to insure this order did not obligate the British government to further ammunition orders from the U.S.A. [6] The number of magazines were specified on February 1, 1940, via a memorandum titled, Initial War Orders: 750 Thompson Guns Model 21 AC, 3000 fifty round drum magazines, 5,000 twenty round box magazines along with 1000 handbooks (handwritten notation). The Initial War Orders (IWO) memorandum was signed by G.W. Turner, the Principal Assistant Secretary (Production) or P.A.S.(P.) at the MoS, for Admiral Harold Brown. [7] These two individuals will be mentioned many times as this story unfolds; both played an integral part with the procurement of the Thompson gun.

On February 1, 1940, the British Supply Board in Canada received official approval to order 750 Model 21A.C. Thompson guns, 3000 drum magazines, 5000 twenty round box magazines and 1000 handbooks. Irrespective of specifying the A.C. or compensator model, it appeared the compensator might not have been included for this initial order - "Compensator could follow reasonable period provided guns suitably finished to take them." [8] While the British bureaucracy had meetings, discussed potential future liabilities and drafted letters, the government of Sweden purchased 500 of the available Thompson guns on January 26, 1940. [9]

---

[2] (WO 185/12) Letter from R.J. Sinclair, Director General of Army Requirements (D.G.A.R.), The War Office to Lt. General Sir Maurice G. Taylor, Senior Military Advisor to the Minister of Supply, dated 19th January, 1940 **(unless otherwise stated, all file references are to WO 185/12)**
[3] CYPHER TELEGRAM CANADA, from Col. J.H.M. Greenly, Controller-General, British Supply Board (BSB) in Canada to Vice-Admiral Harold Brown, Director General of Munitions Production (D.G.M.P.), Ministry of Supply,18th January, 1940
[4] Ministry of Supply (MoS) Memorandum No. 15/40, Exchange Requirements Committee, dated 24th January, 1940
[5] Letter from Treasury Chambers, E.G. Compton, dated 26th January, 1940, to W.M Allen, MoS
[6] Letter from Treasury Chambers, E.G. Compton, dated 31st January, 1940, to W.M Allen, MoS
[7] Initial War Orders for Thompson Sub Machine Guns, (218/1) signed G.W. Turner, P.A.S.(P.), dated February 1, 1940
[8] CYPHER TELEGRAM CANADA, 1February 1940, from Sir Arthur Robinson, MoS, to Col. J.H.M. Greenly, Controller-General, BSB in Canada.
[9] Cable from Sweden to U.S.A. on January 26th setting forth confirmed Swedish order of 500 Thompson guns and accessories, signed, AEROMATERIEL

The Swedish order meant the supply of Thompson guns was all but gone. It is unknown if the British were aware that this small supply of then available Thompson guns were actually the remaining guns from the original 1921/1922 production run of 15,000 guns from Colt's Patent Fire Arms Manufacturing Company. Auto-Ordnance Corporation (AOC) had contracted with Savage Arms in December 1939 to put the Thompson gun back in production but the expected delivery date was several months away. [10]

For reasons unknown, this first British order of 750 guns was actually made in two parts. Notification from the British Supply Board (BSB) in Canada received on February 10th stated that an order for 450 Thompson guns with accessories was placed. The cable requested a decision on packing the ammunition in wooden boxes ($24 per 1000 rounds) or metal lined boxes ($24.50 per thousand rounds). It also advised that the French were contemplating a very large order for "this same material" in a few days. [11] A quick decision was made to pack the first order of ammunition in metal lined boxes. [12]

When AOC received the order for Model 1921AC Thompson guns, it promptly informed the British that it had discontinued the production of the Model 1921AC. The BSB in Canada quickly changed the order to the "Model 28AC with compensator instead." AOC was projecting delivery by the middle of March. Handwritten notations on the telegram include "175 dollars" and "25 dollars more" and indicate that the 21AC fired at 800 rounds a minute but that the 28AC fired at 600 rounds a minute. [13] The change in models was approved with a stated presumption 300 more guns were being ordered to fill the initial order of 750 guns. In addition, instructions were given setting forth the requirement for the "very early delivery" of at least two guns with compensators, three 50 round drums and five 20 round magazines to the Director of Artillery, MoS (who had responsibility for small arms design). [14] These two guns and ancillary equipment were to be used in the fabrication of carrying chests. [15] The BSB in Canada confirmed the complete order of 750 Thompson guns on February 28, 1940. [16]

Two Thompson guns, 8 magazines and 2000 rounds of ammunition including 200 tracer rounds for testing were loaded on the British *M.S. Malayan Prince* in New York harbor on March 14th and were shipped to London. The guns were consigned to the Director of Artillery. [17]

Box magazines and drums were a main topic of discussion as the British slowly adopted the Thompson gun. The initial order of box magazines was increased from 5000 to 8000 and drums from 3000 to 4500 while the official first order was being placed. [18] This increase caused a problem at the Munitions Production Central and it requested on February 3, 1940 that the War Office make a "case" for the expenditure of additional monies. [19] After some correspondence involving the Exchange Requirements Committee of the Treasury and the D.G.M.P., a new order for 1500 drum magazines and 3000 box magazines at a cost of £10,000 was given. [20] The Treasury approved this order on 15th March 1940. [21]

---

[10] Hill, 289-293, 301-306
[11] Cypher Telegram Canada, dated February 10, 1940
[12] CYPHER TELEGRAM, SECRET, undated, from Col. J.H.M. Greenly, BSB, to Sir Arthur Robinson, MoS.
[13] CYPHER TELEGRAM CANADA, from Col. J.H.M. Greenly, to Vice-Admiral Harold Brown, D.G.M.P., dated 15th February, 1940
[14] TELEGRAM dated 25th February, 1940, from Cleverly, Deputy Secretary, MoS, to Col. J.H.M. Greenly,
[15] Internal MoS document, typed notation on Minute Sheet for A.D.(S.A.), dated 20 February 1940
[16] CYPHER TELEGRAM CANADA, from Col. J.H.M. Greenly, to Harold Brown, dated 28th February, 1940
[17] Extract from CYPHER TELEGRAM CANADA, dated 20th March 1940
[18] Handwritten document, Reference Thompson Machine Carbines, A.D.S.A. Gibson, dated January 27, 1940
[19] Typed document dated 2.3.40 [2 MAR 1940] with M.P.c. statement
[20] CYPHER TELEGRAM CANADA, 7 March, 1940, from Sir Arthur Robinson, MoS. to Col. J.H.M. Greenly, BSB
[21] Letter from Treasury Chambers, F.G. Lee, dated 15th March 1940, to W.M Allen, MoS

A telegram on April 9th specified vertical fore grips were wanted on Thompson guns if possible but that shipment should not be delayed if horizontal grips already fitted. Also stated, "Slings not required." [22] Another telegram the next day stated the cost of guns in this shipment was $150 each but the cost would probably drop to between $110 and $130 each if "substantial orders" were placed. The telegram also warned that the Canadians and other sources were ordering Thompson guns. It urged to "cable immediately any further requirements" to take advantage of these potential savings. [23] A push was on to order more Thompsons before the first of the 750 guns arrived.

As the delivery time dragged on for the guns, good news was obtained regarding the ammunition. 500,000 rounds in 259 cases sailed on the _S.S. Georgic_ on April 5th bound for Liverpool. [24] Finally, on April 17th information about the first order of guns was received - "180 guns and spares plus 8020 magazines go forward on _S.S. Eastern Prince_ probably April 16th (sail date of April 16th later confirmed via SECRET cable dated April 19th). The first 182 guns of the first contract were to be equipped with horizontal fore grips but the remainder would have vertical grips. [25] It appears the two Thompson guns previously shipped to Britain on the _M.S. Malayan Prince_ on March 14th also had horizontal fore grips. Based on documented production schedules at Savage Arms, it is very likely these first two Thompson guns were of Colt manufacture. [26]

15 BROAD STREET, NEW YORK   **TELEPHONE HANOVER 2-2460**

BRITISH PURCHASING COMMISSION

The British Purchasing Commission

The British Supply Board (BSB) was a purchasing agency set up in Canada by the MoS in 1939 to purchase munitions from Canadian sources for the war effort. The duties were expanded later that year and it became the British Supply Board in Canada and the United States. It was not a direct purchasing agency; its functions were to coordinate purchasing in Canada and the United States. Canadian orders were coordinated through Canada's Supply Board. American orders were to be managed with the soon to be formed British Purchasing Commission.

The British Purchasing Commission (B.P.C.) was created on November 7, 1939. Under the direction of Arthur B. Purvis, it was responsible for purchasing arms and war supplies from North American manufacturers for the British MoS. Purvis initially found his authority severely lacking because other missions or entities from England could engage in direct purchases of war material without the knowledge or authority of the B.P.C. However, by the middle of 1940 Purvis had extended the authority of the B.P.C. for the purchase of all machine tools, iron and steel and more importantly, to require

---

[22] Draft Telegram, dated 9 April 1940, from Sir Arthur Robinson, MoS to Col. J.H.M. Greenly, BSB
[23] CYPHER TELEGRAM CANADA, from Col. J.H.M. Greenly, in Canada to Harold Brown, dated 10th April, 1940
[24] CYPHER TELEGRAM, CANADA, 9th April 1940, from Col. J.H.M. Greenly, to Sir Arthur Robinson, MoS
[25] CYPHER TELEGRAM, CANADA, 16th April 1940, from Col. J.H.M. Greenly, to Sir Arthur Robinson, MoS
[26] Frank Iannamico, _American Thunder II_ (Nevada: Moose Lake Publishing), 165

complete and detailed reports from all other purchasing bodies. [27]   The French government was also active at this time in the United States making purchases of American goods for their war effort. Soon after the creation of the B.P.C., the British and French governments coordinated their purchases with the creation of the Anglo-French Coordinating Commission under Jean Monnet in London and the Anglo-French Purchasing Board under Arthur Purvis in the United States. This partnership prevented manufacturers of war materiel from pitting one country against another in separate negotiations regarding price, quantity, delivery, etc.

Russell Maguire

On April 8, 1940, the President of Auto-Ordnance Corporation (AOC), Russell Maguire, sent a letter to Mr. Leslie Burgin, the Minister of Supply for the British Government. Maguire noted in the opening sentence that Britain had made comments in the American press of their concern for the time involved in the production and delivery of small arms. He went on to confirm the shipment of the two Thompson guns in March 1940 to the MoS and how, "this gun is standard equipment of the armed forces of the United States…" He then recounted how the French to date have ordered 6,000 guns of which 3000 [28] have been delivered; ending with how AOC had received a small order from the British Government. He boasted, "Our tooling is complete and these guns are coming off the assembly line daily." Maguire then delivered the main purpose of the letter by promising "prompt deliveries" of Thompson guns if AOC had "an indication of your future requirement on this gun." This information would allow AOC "to more efficiently quicken our production" and "stock the necessary raw materials, etc." Maguire ended the letter by stating - "If orders were placed with us now, we believe that we could furnish approximately 10,000 of these weapons within the next 90 days…" [29]

What Maguire didn't say was AOC had to pay Savage Arms for the production of 10,000 Thompson guns (the initial AOC order with Savage Arms) regardless of sales. [30] His boast of guns coming off the assembly line daily probably occurred about the time this letter was received as production deliveries began around mid-April. [31] However, it would take Savage Arms 120 days to manufacture 10,000 Thompson guns. [32]

While the military and civilian bureaucrats demonstrated a great ability on how to create paperwork, they knew the war was not going well for Britain in the spring of 1940. More Thompson guns would be

---

[27] Entry by H. Duncan Hall on Arthur Purvis in *Oxford Dictionary of National Biography,* http://www.oxforddnb.com/view/article/35635
[28] These 3000 would be of Colt's manufacture – *The Ultimate Thompson Book,* Hill (Albert), 283-289
[29] Letter from Russell Maguire to Edward Leslie Burgin, Minister of Supply, dated April 8, 1940
[30] Hill, 301-303
[31] President's Report to Stockholders, Thompson Automatic Arms Corporation, AOC, dated March 17, 1941
[32] Iannamico, 165

needed, most likely many many more. Officers in the MoS and BSB pressed for making additional orders to obtain better pricing but no approval was given. [33] However, some were optimistic more Thompson guns would be procured and the order was given to explore projected deliveries and prices. [34] AOC was interested in supplying more guns to Britain but needed specifics as to actual numbers required over what time period before quoting prices. AOC did make known they had other commitments. [35] What AOC may not have known is the British military were looking at other submachine guns.

from the book *"TOMMY"* by Auto-Ordnance Vice-President Frederic A. Willis
Russell Maguire, President of Auto-Ordnance Corporation, admiring a finely crafted silver miniature presentation Thompson submachine gun. One of these miniatures was presented to Winston Churchill later in the war. [36]

The Second Order

Just when it appeared Russell Maguire's letter had been ignored, the British placed a new order on May 14th for 2000 more guns, 12,000 rounds of ammunition for each gun, 12,000 drum magazines, 20,000 box magazines and spares parts in the ratio as ordered previously. The sentence toward the end of the telegram told the complete story - "Delivery very urgent." [37] Two days later notification was received

---

[33] Telegram, SECRET, dated 18 April 1940, from Sir Arthur Robinson, MoS to Col. J.H.M. Greenly, BSB

[34] Telegram, SECRET, dated 4 May 1940, from [O.S.] Cleverly, Deputy Secretary, MoS to Col. J.H.M. Greenly

[35] CYPHER TELEGRAM, CANADA, 9 May 1940, from Col. J.H.M. Greenly, to Robinson and Cleverly

[36] Hill, 425

[37] Telegram, "Most Immediate," dated 14 May 1940, from Sir Arthur Robinson, MoS to Col. J.H.M. Greenly

that delivery of this order of Thompson guns was "promised" between June 21st and July 10th; delivery of 24 million rounds of ammunition "promised" in June, July and August (1940). [38] G.W. Turner, the Principal Assistant Secretary (Production) or P.A.S.(P.), MoS, signed the Initial War Orders memorandum for 2000 Thompson guns and associated equipment, dated May 14, 1940, for the D.G.M.P. Director General of Munitions (Production). [39]

Gun Firm Moving To Utica, N.Y.

Auto Ordnance Corp., Maker of Thompson Weapon Praised by British, Leaves City

The Auto Ordance Corporation, owner of patents on Thompson Automatic Guns which an English military expert in the London press Friday declared "ideal" for use against German parachute troops, has moved its Hartford office to Utica, New York.

Samuel M. Stone, president of Colt's Patent Fire Arms Manufacturing Company which made a quantity of the guns for the firm some years ago, said the corporation began to pull up local stakes about May 1 in order to be located near the Savage Arms Company in Utica which is now manufacturing them. Orders for the guns are placed through the Auto Ordnance Corporation.

George E. Goll of Maplewood Avenue, West Hartford, who has managed the local office, has also moved to Utica.

Briton Wants Weapon.

According to the Associated Press, Lieutenant Colonel T. A. Lowe, the London Daily Mail's military correspondent, has stated that Thompson Automatic Guns are just the thing to use against the parachute troops and has urged, in an orticle, that the British Government place a rush order. "There must be a large supply of these Thompson automatic guns in America. No time should be lost in cabling an order for a supply," Colonel Lowe wrote, according to the Associated Press. Mr. Stone said Saturday that, as far as he knows, there is not a large supply of the guns available at present. The U. S. War Department placed a $435,000 order for them last August.

Colonel Lowe was reported as attacking the organization of British defense volunteers and urging that the whole plan be scrapped. "There is widespread uneasiness that once again we are trusting to ancient weapons to guard against a modern menace," he said in his article.

The Hartford office of the Auto Ordnance Corporation was located in the South Meadows on Sequassen Street. Its main office is in New York City.

An undated and unidentified newspaper clipping from the May 1940 period from the personal scrapbook of Russell Maguire highlights the British interest in the American Thompson submachine gun. The supply of Thomson guns manufactured by Colt's years ago has been depleted and Savage Arms of Utica, New York, is the new subcontractor for Auto-Ordnance Corporation (AOC). George E. Goll, now the AOC Chief Engineer, has moved to Utica to oversee the Savage production. Note the comments by the British Officer regarding the Local Defense Volunteers, the forerunner to the Home Guard.

---

[38] CYPHER TELEGRAM, CANADA, 16th May 1940, from Col. J.H.M. Greenly, to Robinson, MoS and Cleverly
[39] Initial War Orders for Thompson Sub Machine Guns, signed G.W. Turner, P.A.S.(P.), dated May 14, 1940

The Third Order

What happened three days after the second order indicated the British were finally on-board with General Thompson's trench broom - "order immediately Thompson Guns twenty six thousand two hundred and fifty." Included in this order were 57 million rounds of ammunition, 415,000 box magazines, 185,000 drum magazines and spare parts. [40]

The First Order: Thompson Guns are being shipped!

Shortly after the third order was placed information was received in Britain that 200 more Thompson guns from the first order had sailed from New York on May 18th on board the *S.S. Northern Prince*. Included in this shipment were 3044 drum magazines, 1500 handbooks, 450 firing pin springs and 450 trigger springs. [41]

On May 23rd additional information was received that updated the number of drum magazines to 4544 shipped with the 200 Thompson guns on the *S.S. Northern Prince*, above. Expected delivery was May 29th. It also forecast the shipment of 150 more guns and 1,000,000 rounds of ammunition on the *S.S. Argos* sailing May 23rd and the remaining 218 guns on the *S.S. British Prince* sailing May 27, 1940. [42]

It took five shipments (March 14th – 2 guns, April 16th – 180 guns, May 18th – 200 guns, May 23rd – 150 guns and May 27th – 218 guns) to deliver the first 750 Thompson guns to Great Britain, the last guns most likely arriving during the first of June 1940. Of course, upon arrival from America, the cargo had to be off loaded, inspected and transported to the desired location for training and issuance. The Thompson gun in Great Britain would begin having a big impact during the second half of 1940.

The First Military Action

The first known use of the Thompson gun by the British military is documented in an internal MoS handwritten memorandum dated January 20, 1940. This communication details the particulars of the first order of 750 guns and three million rounds of ammunition. The information concerning ammunition is most noteworthy - "Messrs. I.C.I. Ltd. are now working on a small order for such ammunition for the few guns now with B.E.F. but I understand are doing so at the detriment of their pistol ammunition production. I therefore assume this 3 million and any further supplies will have to come from U.S.A." I.C.I. Ltd or the Imperial Chemical Industries conglomerate was a household name in Great Britain during World War II. It controlled nearly all the explosives and propellant industries in Britain and operated several government small arms ammunition plants. ICI ammunition under the brand names of Eley and Kynoch are known around the world.

The British Expeditionary Force (BEF) arrived in France in September 1939, well before the War Office placed the first order of Thompson guns. The question arises as to how and where the BEF obtained a "few" Thompson guns. The answer is found in the records of the Ordnance Board, a joint service board of munitions experts that advised the British military on weapons. Proceedings of the Ordnance Board, No. 3,947, dated December 22, 1939, acknowledged, "A demand has been received from B.E.F. for an immediate supply of machine carbines or gangster guns. The Board has investigated many of these

---

[40] CYPHER Telegram, "Most Immediate," dated 17 May 1940, from Robinson, MoS to Col. J.H.M. Greenly
[41] Handwritten Extract from Cable from Col. J.H.M. Greenly, to Sir Arthur Robinson, MoS, dated May 21, 1940
[42] Letter from R.J. Sinclair, D.G.A.R., War Office, to G.W. Turner, P.A.S.(P.), MoS, dated May 23, 1940

weapons during the past few years but beyond a number of samples we possess no stock of such guns and will be compelled to buy what we can find. Seven sample guns have been sent to B.E.F. and we shall buy some more as soon as we can. Future demands and any possible production will depend upon the experience obtained at the front." This report did not specifically identify the seven sample guns, however, the American Thompson gun was referenced several times in the document, including the statement, "Messrs. B.S.A. Guns Ltd. were the agents for the Thompson sub-machine guns…" [43]

All doubt regarding the identity of the "few" or sample weapons was removed in Proceedings of the Ordnance Board, No. 4,450, dated January 24, 1940 - "Regarding the Thompson machine carbine. Six of these weapons are now undergoing troop trials with B.E.F. It must be noted that this weapon is the most costly of its class that we know of; it costs over £50 per gun and involves us in the problem of the dollar exchange. Also, it is the most complicated and elaborate as regards manufacture, and, therefore, probably as regards spares and maintenance. From a shooting aspect, it tends to shoot high unless fitted with a special muzzle compensator which costs another 20 dollars. With these disadvantages it still is only a machine carbine weapon with corresponding limitations of range and accuracy." [44] The seventh sample gun was not identified.

A reading of both reports leaves little doubt the Ordnance Board was not impressed with the Thompson gun from a cost and manufacturing standpoint. Other submachine guns under review by the Board included the Hungarian Kiraly and the Finish Suomi. The Suomi was deemed "the best of all the machine carbines" but was "unobtainable." The Thompson gun, "the least desirable of all on technical grounds, was likely to be available." A decision was reached "to adopt the 0.45 inch Thompson to meet immediate needs." [45] This early use of a non-standard weapon and ammunition readily demonstrated the resolve of the British military in the early days of the war.

These six Thompson sample guns caused the "small order" of .45 caliber ammunition to be contracted for at I.C.I. Ltd. Additional internal MoS documentation dated January 22, 1920 revealed the following prices for .45 caliber ammunition - "ICI price is £4-5 a 1000" compared to "(say) £8 – 1000" from US sources. [46] The Thompson guns sent to the BEF would have been of Colt's manufacture. That the British military had a small inventory of sample Thompson guns in late 1939 or the beginning of 1940 is not surprising. AOC was only too glad to sell or supply potential customers with sample guns for testing purposes. The British military would have been a prime potential customer. U.S. government export records show 21 Thompson guns exported to England (some records cite B.S.A. Ltd, Birmingham by name) between 1921 and 1925. [47] There had also been a number of Thompson guns captured from the Irish Republican Army (IRA) by British forces in Ireland prior to 1940. [48]

Documentation of historical events is always best preserved with pictures. Written documentation always leads to more questions; pictures make believers. A visit to the BEF's stationed on the Maginot Line in France by King George VI on December 9, 1939 was certainly a newsworthy event. What better place or person to show off one of the new "sample" or gangster guns. It is not surprising the King and the Thompson gun were photographed together on that winter day in France. What is remarkable is the picture does not seem to have been widely circulated.

---

[43] Proceedings of the Ordnance Board, No. 3,947, dated 22.12.39

[44] Proceedings of the Ordnance Board, No. 4,450, dated 24.1.40

[45] Ibid

[46] Internal MoS documentation (5), dated 22.1.1940

[47] Gordon Herigstad, *Colt Thompson Serial Numbers*, 3rd Edition (Privately Printed), Exported Thompsons: 1-3

[48] Patrick Jung, "The Thompson submachine gun during and after the Anglo-Irish war: the new evidence," *The Irish Sword*, Vol. XXI, (Winter 1998, No. 84), 209-212

King George VI visited his forces and a sector of the Maginot Line in December 1939.

from the collection of the Operation Dynamo War Museum, Dunkerque, France

A picture on display at the Operation Dynamo War Museum in Dunkerque, France titled, "King George VI visited his forces and a sector of the Maginot Line in December 1939." The source of the picture is unknown but it is believed to have been taken from a then current publication. The Thompson gun shown in the picture does not have a compensator and is equipped with a 50 round drum. The drum is empty because the actuator or cocking knob is in the forward position. Obviously, the weapon was made safe for King George VI to handle. The Thompson could be either a Model of 1921A or a Model of 1928A. It is definitely of Colt manufacture and most likely one of the six "sample" Thompson guns supplied to the BEF. The two soldiers on the left appear to be senior French officers.

Another source of Thompson guns for British soldiers in France would be the 3000 guns previously mentioned that were purchased by the French government in November 1939. Could the British have borrowed a few of these guns? While this is possible, it would have been after February 1940. Recently discovered British Supply Council records titled, U.S. WARTIME EXPORTS TO FRANCE, revealed the first exports of firearms and ammunition to France did not begin until February 1940. The dollar value of "Firearms and Ammunition" exported to France in February 1940 was only $6,000, but increased to $258,000 in March 1940. Source documentation listed for this information is the U.S. Department of Commerce. [49]

The use of the Thompson gun by the BEF had a direct impact on the first order of Thompson guns and equipment. Internal documentation at the MoS revealed, "The original estimate of magazines requirements has been condemned by BEF and extra has been demanded..." [50] Note the strong language with use of the word *condemned*. It leaves no doubt in the minds of bureaucrats. The initial increase in drum and box magazines orders referenced earlier (p. 3) may be directly attributed to experiences by the BEF in France. An Initial War Order memorandum or IWO was issued for 1500 additional 50 round drums and 3,000 additional 20 round box magazines on March 14, 1940. [51]

---

[49] (AVIA 38/1098) Table from British Supply Council regarding exports to France, dated 1941
[50] Internal MoS documentation 25) by A.F. Dobie-Bateman, Treasury, dated March 7, 1940
[51] Initial War Order, Thompson Sub. Machine Gun Magazines, (218/4) signed G.W. Turner, P.A.S.(P.), March 14, 1941

Geoffrey Keating, Imperial War Museum collection
An officer of the 52nd Lowland Division poses with his Thompson sub-machine gun and a Bedford MWD truck in France, 13 June 1940. While the picture may have been posed, this soldier is ready for action. Note the vertical fore grip, the position of the actuator (cocking knob) in the rear or cocked position and the compensator at the end of the barrel.

All doubts of the Thompson gun being with the BEF in France disappeared when army photographer Geoffrey Keating took a picture on June 13, 1940, that documented the British military acted very quickly in getting the Thompson gun to the front lines of the battle with Germany. While the evacuation at the port of Dunkirk in northern France removed much of the British Expeditionary Force, several combat units and a large number of support personnel were trapped south of German military forces. A "second" British Expeditionary Force (BEF) was sent to the western part of France during the Dunkirk evacuation to assist the French army in establishing a secure foothold in France. This strategy was soon abandoned. A new plan, named Operation Ariel, was to evacuate as many Allied soldiers and as much equipment as possible to Great Britain. The 52nd Lowland Division was a part of this second BEF. Photographic archives at the Imperial War Museum in London reveal Keating took many pictures on June 13, 1940; one is captioned, "A soldier of the 52nd Lowland Division poses with his Thompson sub-machine gun and a Bedford MWD truck in France, 13 June 1940." Of particular note is the vertical fore grip. This may indicate the Thompson gun was one of the early "sample" Thompson guns with the BEF or from the second shipment of guns (shipped from USA on May 18th) from the first 750 Thompson gun order. Other possibilities include some of the Thompson guns in the first shipment arrived with vertical fore grips or the fore grip was changed (a very simple procedure).

France Surrenders!

A SECRET letter from R.J. Sinclair, Deputy General Army Requirements (D.G.A.R.), War Office, to G.W. Turner, P.A.S.(P.), MoS, dated May 18, 1940, was one of the first documents to reference the B.P.C. It also cited the third order of Thompson guns, above and stated in part:

> "As I dare say you know the telegram from Monnet to Purvis which was agreed at a meeting on Wednesday night when Mr. Cleverly [Deputy Secretary, MoS] was present, referred, inter alia, to Thompson Sub-Machine Guns and stated that it was almost certain that we could take delivery of all the quantities likely to be available. This does not, of course, bind us and the telegram was mainly concerned with the endeavour to extract from America as much as possible of these and other equipments we urgently require and to get them as quickly as possible. If by any chance we find that America can supply a larger quantity than the 26,000 quickly we might have to think again because the French might be glad to have any surplus. Meantime, the specific enquiry you have made from the Mission would give Purvis a definite idea of the quantity required for British Service purposes." [52]

The French were very active in the purchase of the Thompson. A June 17th telegram from Purvis to Monet referenced an order of 25,000 Thompson guns and how negotiations were underway "to bridge deliveries before the end of the year." In addition, the French were told a capital expenditure of $525,000 would increase production of the Thompson gun from 7,200 to 16,000 monthly by October 1940. [53]

Unfortunately for the Allied forces, France would surrender to Germany within days and not be in a position to benefit from any extra capacity in Thompson production. However, the purchasing partnerships formed by Arthur Purvis and Jean Monet proved extremely valuable to Great Britain after the fall of France in June 1940. Without this relationship, the new French government under control of Germany may have been able to deny the British all war materials contracted for by the French government. While the French government was in the process of arranging an armistice with Germany, officials from both organizations met in New York to discuss the situation. Colonel Jacquin, head of the French Air Commission, was in charge of the negotiations for the French government. He had one condition - "You must take all the French contracts or none of them. You cannot pick our bones after we have fallen." Condition accepted; legal documents were quickly drafted allowing Great Britain to assume control of all the French contracts. [54]

The Fourth Order

Very few Thompson guns had actually arrived in Britain and been put in service when authorization on June 13th was given to "double" the third order if the manufacturer could offer improved deliveries. The urgency was evident as this authorization contained a request to look for other sources of the Thompson gun in America. [55] On June 17th the BSB in Canada reported an additional order of 26,250 guns, 407,000 box magazines, 26,500 drum magazines, "usual spares," and 57 million rounds of ammunition was made. Delivery of guns was at 700 per week in June, expected to increase to 2800 weekly by middle of September and 4000 weekly by middle of October (1940). [56]

---

[52] SECRET letter from R.J. Sinclair, D.G.A.R., War Office, to G.W. Turner, P.A.S.(P.), MoS, dated May 18, 1940

[53] Extract from telegram from Purvis to Monnet, dated 17th June 1940

[54] E.R. Stettinius, Jr., *Lend Lease, Weapon For Victory* (New York: Macmillan, 1944), 31

[55] Telegram, 13 June 1940, from Sir Arthur Robinson, MoS to Col. J.H.M. Greenly

[56] CYPHER TELEGRAM, CANADA, 17th June 1940, from Col. J.H.M. Greenly, to Sir Arthur Robinson, MoS

This fourth order initially caused a lot of confusion. The BSB in Canada, when setting forth the delivery schedule of the 28,250 guns initially on order (2000 + 26250), reported - "The total quantity of Thompson Guns and ammunition actually ordered in U.S.A. is not clear from telegram received…" and requested "exact information on this subject." The BSB added the following information - "The 28250 Guns is in addition to the 750 already shipped." [57] What followed was an order by the MoS for an accounting of guns, magazines and ammunition on June 22, 1940. [58] The immediate reply was "Thompson Sub Machine gun capacity now fully booked by us till end of 1940." [59] The complete answer listed the total number of guns and associated equipment on order as follows: [60]

> 55,250 guns
> 862,040 box magazines
> 469,600 drum magazines
> 141 million rounds of ammunition

The author of this report, signature illegible, stated the 55,250 Thompson guns on order are "exclusive of the original order of 750 guns already delivered." [61] Simple math indicates otherwise: 2,000 + 26250 + 26250 = 54500. You must add in the first order of 750 Thompson guns to reach 55,250, the total number of guns ordered to date. A similar mistake is also present in the MoS ledger books detailing the purchase of the Thompson gun for the British Military. The ledger actually lists the correct number of guns ordered as 55,250 in June 1940, but then adds back in the original order of 750 guns to reach a total of 56,000 guns. [62] The Initial War Orders memorandum, used to account for the third and fourth orders, specified 55,250 Thompson guns. The memorandum notating the 55,250 figure did include the previous order of 2000 Thompson guns and actually cancelled the IWO memorandum for that order. [63] Apparently, no one recognized the mistakes involving the double count of the initial order of 750 guns – which seemed to give everyone an accounting problem. However, counting and accounting problems would be the norm for the Thompson gun!

Another telegram regarding the search to find additional sources of new Thompson guns included instructions to look for stocks of used or "second hand" guns. [64] Inquiries to this effect resulted in an intercepted cable that stated new Thompson guns were available at $218 each with a fifty round drum or $200 with a twenty round box magazine directly from Auto-Ordnance Corporation, 80 Broadway (New York). [65] The B.P.C. evaluated the intercepted cable and responded that AOC was quoting their highest price because of a third party inquiry for Thompson guns. The B.P.C. was paying $140 each per Thompson gun compared to the quoted $218 price. In addition, the B.P.C. was paying $22.50 per thousand rounds of ammunition versus the quoted price of $32. The B.P.C. ended their response by stating they have contracted for the entire output of Thompson production until the end of the year (1940). [66]

[57] Telegram 270/S.A./6.) to D.D.A.R. from A. J. Manson, dated June 21, 1940
[58] Telegram, 22 June 1940, from Sir Arthur Robinson, MoS to Col. J.H.M. Greenly
[59] Handwritten Extract from cable dated June 23, 1940
[60] CYPHER TELEGRAM, CANADA, 24th June 1940, from Col. J.H.M. Greenly, to Sir Arthur Robinson, MoS
[61] Telegram 270/SA/6, to D.G.M.P., dated June 26, 1940
[62] Ministry of Supply MoS), SUPP 4-310 – Contract Record Books: THOMPSON SUB-MACHINE GUNS
[63] Initial War Orders for Thompson Sub Machine Guns… (218/6), signed G.W. Turner, P.A.S.(P.), dated May 27, 1940
[64] Telegram, 25 June 1940, from Sir Arthur Robinson, MoS to Col. J.H.M. Greenly
[65] CYPHER TELEGRAM CANADA, 5th July 1940
[66] TELEGRAM, for MoS from British Purchasing Commission (B.P.C.), dated 9Jul1940

'The War Illustrated,' July 19th, 1940   Registered at the G.P.O. as a Newspaper

Vol. 3 ★ HOW FRANCE'S WARSHIPS WERE SAVED FROM HITLER ★ No. 46

THE WAR ILLUSTRATED

3d Weekly

Edited by
SIR JOHN HAMMERTON
Editor of 'THE WAR ILLUSTRATED' (1914-1920)
'WORLD WAR, 1914-1918,' 'I WAS THERE!' etc.

He is Ready to Deal with 'Gangster' Invaders

The cover of *The War Illustrated*, a British publication devoted to stories about the war, dated July 19, 1940. The Thompson gun in the hands of a British soldier is most likely from the first British order of 750 Thompson guns. Note the horizontal fore grip, Kerr sling with British broad arrow marking and compensator on the end of the barrel.

14

The French Thompson Guns

The British decision to assume all the French contracts in the USA paid immediate benefits. A telegram from Arthur Purvis to Jean Monet on June 21, 1940, directly references "about 1200 Thompson Submachine Guns and 5 million cartridges" purchased by the French that "might be of immediate use in North Africa." [67] The 1200 Thompson guns were actually 1150 guns in 115 cases, one case of slings and 400,000 rounds of ammunition in 200 cases. [68] The Thompson guns, ammunition and accessories were loaded on the *S.S. San Marcos* and shipped from New York the week of July 9, 1940. [69]

The Second Order: Thompson Guns are being shipped!

Information was received on July 8th that all 2000 guns from the second order would be "completed" on July 10th. It was further reported 160 guns were ready now and would be shipped the following week. 12,050 magazines were shipped on June 21st and July 2nd. [70] A handwritten undated document titled, "Thompson Machine Gun Arrivals" indicated the first order of 750 guns arrived safely. Another 2470 guns, including the 1150 guns from the French order shipped on the *S.S. San Marcos*, had arrived with an additional 1120 to 1340 guns "in transit." The probable time frame of this document is late July or August 1940. [71]

MINISTRY, HARROGATE 6471

ONE:
Extn...... 1021......

ommunications on the
of this letter should
essed to:—

UNDER SECRETARY
ATE, AIR MINISTRY,

AIR MINISTRY,

DEPT. ZA,

HARROGATE,

YORKS.

The Air Ministry

With orders of 55,250 guns since February 1940 and deliveries starting to be scheduled on a more predictive basis, the Thompson gun had found a place with the British Military. The Air Ministry wanted its share of Thompson guns and contacted the MoS with several letters requesting 12,000 guns. The Air Ministry understood that the MoS had contracted for the total production of Thompson guns in 1940 from America. It wanted to know if their request for 12,000 guns could be satisfied out of the 1940 production, believed by them to be 50,000 guns, or if they needed to submit their order for 12,000 guns after the completion of the current contracts. [72]

---

[67] Telegram from Mr. Purvis to Mr. Monnet, dated June 21, 1940 – CAB 85/14, PURCO NO. 236 (IN)

[68] NO 66 Suply memorandum, handwritten, for MoS from Purchasing Commission, dated 22 July 1940

[69] CYPHER TELEGRAM CANADA, 9th July 1940

[70] CYPHER TELEGRAM CANADA, 8th July 1940

[71] Handwritten undated document, "Thompson Machine Gun Arrivals" - probable July/August time frame

[72] Letter from Deputy General of Equipment, Air Ministry, to Secretary, MoS, dated 30th July 1940

No Additional Orders?

When engaged in a war of survival, planning for the future is paramount. On August 16, 1940, the Acting Consul General in New York cabled the Minister of Supply with questions about munitions procurement in 1941. The telegram references Thompson gun procurement of 54,000 guns with production rising to 4,000 guns weekly in December. It also references the procurement of 21,000 "Smith W." (Smith & Wesson carbines) 9mm guns with production rising to 1,800 guns weekly in November. The telegram stresses the importance of obtaining permission to continue contracting for guns and ammunition in 1941. [73] On August 28th another cable was sent that stated the "Thompson and Smith and Wesson Companies" are "pressing us" for decisions on additional orders for 1941 or they will contract with others for their 1941 capacity. [74] On August 30th the Deputy Director, Army Requirements, sent a letter to the P.A.S.(P.), MoS, espousing the same problem. This letter referenced how the Deputy General Army Requirements (D.G.A.R.) is aware the Schmeisser gun may be placed in production in Britain. However, the pressing issue is being able to retain the American production capacity without further orders. The only potential future order pending before the Treasury was an order of 10,000 Thompson guns for the Royal Air Force. [75] The Schmeisser gun mentioned above and later in this story is believed to be the Schmeisser MP28/II submachine gun. It is better known in Britain as the Lanchester submachine gun, a very close copy of German Schmeisser MP-28 submachine gun. It was developed by George H. Lanchester and manufactured by Sterling Engineering Co between 1941 and 1945. It was issued to the British Navy and Marines.

Army Training Memorandum No.35

The British army was not idle while waiting on the MoS to place more orders for the Thompson submachine gun. Enough guns had been received, issued and used in combat to show the Thompson gun was an effective killing machine. The following extract from Army Training Memorandum No.35, issued August 1940, highlighted many positive attributes:

> 22. THOMPSON SUB-MACHINE GUN
> The Thompson sub-machine gun is the gangster gun of the American films. Its light weight and ease of handling make it very suitable for engaging opportunity targets at short range and the heavy bullet gives it great stopping power.
> The gun is essentially a weapon for dealing with targets which make their appearance suddenly, when the ordinary rifle or L.M.G. would be handicapped because they are, by comparison, slower to come into action. Such targets might be enemy patrols met at close quarters, enemy caught in ambush at short range, or the clearing of a trench or dug-out.
> The small size of the weapon makes it easy to use in a confined space where larger weapons would be difficult to operate. The fact that it can be easily fired from the hip on the move makes it a useful weapon in the last stages of the assault. It is essentially an offensive weapon.
> As with all automatic weapons, care must be taken to avoid waste of ammunition. It should not be used when the rifle or L.M.G. will answer the purpose equally well. [76]

---

[73] CYPHER TELEGRAM NEW YORK, from the Acting Consul General, dated 16 August 1940
[74] CYPHER TELEGRAM NEW YORK, from the Consul General, dated 29 August 1940
[75] Letter from G.W. Turner, P.A.S.(P.), MoS, to Brigadier D.R.D. Fisher, War Office, dated 30th August 1940
[76] (WO231/251) Army Training Memorandum No.35, August 30, 1940

from the Alan David collection, Australia

An undated news photograph believed to have been taken circa July 1940 showing British troops training with the newly purchased American gangster guns. Again, note the horizontal fore grip. These three Thompson guns are most likely from the first shipment of 180 guns to arrive in Britain. Note the horizontal fore grips and compensators; a British broad arrow marking appears visible on Kerr sling on left.

The Fifth Order

On September 17, 1940, authorization was given to order 17,000 more Thompson guns, 270,000 box magazines, 174,000 drum magazines, 78 million rounds of ammunition, 17,000 gun chests and spare parts at the same rate as previously ordered. [77] Two days later detailed information concerning this order specified 5,000 of these 17,000 Thompson guns are "for India." Also specified for India are 30,000 box magazines, 18,000 drum magazines, 42 million rounds of ammunition and 5,000 gun chests. [78]

The Sixth Order

On October 3, 1940, authorization was given to order "27,000 Guns without repeat without compensator," 166,000 drum magazines, 322,000 box magazines, 27 million rounds of ammunition and spares at the same rate as previously ordered. The order stated that deliveries of this order were expected at a rate of 8,000 guns a month upon completion of current orders. [79] G.W. Turner (for the D.G.M.P.) signed the Initial War Orders memorandum, dated October 8, 1940. [80]

---

[77] CYPHER TELEGRAM NEW YORK, to the Consul General, dated 17th September, 1940
[78] Initial War Orders for Thompson Sub Machine Guns…[218/7], signed G.W. Turner, P.A.S.(P.), dated September 19, 1940
[79] CYPHER TELEGRAM NEW YORK, to the Consul General, dated 3rd October 1940
[80] Initial War Orders for Thompson Sub Machine Guns…[218/8], signed G.W. Turner, P.A.S.(P.), dated October 8, 1940

This telegram was followed up with another Cypher Telegram on October 9, 1940, that read, in part, "Compensators not required for 17,000 ordered. Reference all Thompson guns under current contracts. Please arrange so far as commitments and progress of manufacture allow to omit compensators from future deliveries and arranging appropriate reduction in cost on account of this modification." [81] The reference to the 17,000 Thompson guns was for the fifth order, above. What followed established Savage Arms manufactured the Model of 1928A (without compensator) Thompson as an actual production model. [82]

Photograph by Clive McPherson, Great Britain

Model of 1928A Thompson submachine gun, Serial Number S-17359, manufactured by Savage Arms, Utica, New York, during World War II. Note how S-17359 is not equipped with a compensator (at the end of the barrel). Inset is the left side receiver markings. This early Savage Thompson is on public display as part of the Donnington Collection at the Combined Services Military Collection at Maldon in England.

There is an indication early on that AOC was not happy with the deletion of the compensator from all existing orders of the Thompson gun. There is a reference to an October 13, 1940, Suply 105 telegram where AOC apparently refused to make a price reduction for the deletion of the compensator. Unfortunately, this October 13th telegram, referenced several times in other telegrams, was not found in the available documentation. [83] However, any mysteries regarding the sudden interest in the compensator were explained in a telegram dated November 5, 1940 - "Price of Thompson sub machine gun with compensator on previous orders was 146 dollars and 67 cents and without compensator 130 dollars. Price now quote of 120 dollars therefore represents reduction of 26 dollars and 67 cents if we place order for guns with compensators and reduction of 10 dollars per gun if we accept proposed price of 120 dollars without compensators." [84] Previous orders? The British had specifically ordered or specified the Thompson gun with and without compensators at different prices, taken delivery of both variations and were now price shopping. A telegram dated October 30, 1940, referenced an early price quote from AOC of $130 dollars for a Thompson gun with compensator. The allowance for a compensator was shown to be $16.67. Now with the new quote of $120 for a Thompson gun with compensator the British believed a Thompson without a compensator "ought not to exceed dollars 110 at the most." [85]

---

[81] CYPHER TELEGRAM NEW YORK, 9th October 1940
[82] Tom Davis, Jr., "Savage Arms Model of 1928A," *Small Arms Review*, Vol. 17 No. 3, 47-54
[83] CYPHER TELEGRAM NEW YORK, 18th October 1940
[84] CYPHER TELEGRAM NEW YORK, 5th November 1940
[85] CYPHER TELEGRAM NEW YORK, 1 November 1940

The November 5th telegram also included the following declaration from AOC that is in agreement with the missing October 13th cable, above - "Manufacturer is firm that he will make no price reductions below 120 dollars with or without compensators." The British were quick to do the math. "Proposition as submitted to us means we can obtain 79,000 compensators for approximately $400,000 dollars i.e. 25,000 compensators on existing orders and 54,000 compensators on orders about to be placed." [86] This equates to approximately $5.06 a compensator.

What followed were a series of telegrams about canceling the previous orders to delete the compensator from present and future orders. The issue was finally resolved on November 13, 1940, with a simple telegram stating, "compensators to be supplied on all guns ordered." [87] And the going price for a cash-and-carry Tommy gun with compensator for British forces was now $120 apiece.

Efforts to drive down the cost of the Thompson gun would continue. Cash and carry was not free; every dollar was important. As stated earlier, the British knew their financial resources were finite so they acted accordingly. Little did they know what lay ahead.

It is unknown how many 1928A models were actually manufactured by Savage Arms. The percentage is probably very small seeing how the compensator became standard equipment with all British orders in November 1940. Production records reveal Savage Arms had only manufactured 33,874 Thompson guns by the end of November 1940. [88] All known surviving examples are early Savage guns. Thompson 1928A models found in World War II photographs without serial number information also appear to be early Savage guns based on the date of the photograph or publication.

Imperial War Museum collection by Lt. W.T. Lockeyear: Portrait of a soldier from No. 3 Commando armed with a 'Tommy gun' and wearing a balaclava, at Largs in Scotland, dated 2 May 1942. Note how the Thompson gun is not equipped with a compensator.

[86] CYPHER TELEGRAM NEW YORK, 5th November 1940
[87] CYPHER TELEGRAM NEW YORK, 13th November 1940
[88] Iannamico, 165

The excellent quality of the negative of Lt Lockeyear's picture allowed for the blow-up picture of the right side of the Thompson receiver. The New York address markings on Savage Thompsons are unique: New York, N.Y. U.S.A. Also note the *patent date* markings on the right side of the receiver. Patent date markings on Savage manufactured Thompson guns have only been observed on the first Auto-Ordnance order with Savage Arms (10,000 guns). This is a very early Savage Model of 1928A Thompson.

SMALL ARMS TRAINING, VOLUME I,
PAMPHLET No. 21

THE MACHINE CARBINE

GENERAL NOTES

1. **Object.**—The sole object of weapon training is to teach all ranks the most efficient way of handling their weapons in order to kill the enemy. Instructors will always bear this fact in mind and will continually impress it upon those whom they instruct.

2. **General description.**

Thompson Machine Carbine.—Calibre : ·45 in. Weight : 10 lb. approx. (Plate 1).

Sten Machine Carbine.—Calibre : 9 mm. (·35 in.). Weight : 6½ lb. approx. (Plate 2).

A search of British manuals on the Model 1928 Thompson found many drawings of guns with and without compensators. The 1944 Small Arms Training, Volume 1, Pamphlet No. 21, THE MACHINE CARBINE, features several pictures of Model 1928 Thompson guns with and without compensators. The cover of the 1940 version of this training pamphlet is pictured (p. 81) in the Home Guard chapter.

PLATE 1

PLATE 2

1—22277

LEFT: The first page of the 1944 training manual with a picture of a Thompson and Sten "Machine Carbine" as these guns were often called. Note the position of the sling swivels and sling on the Thompson. It was very common for British armourers to re-position the sling swivels to the top of the butt stock and the side of the fore grip. The Model of 1928 Thompson gun, with and without compensator, served side by side in military operations. No evidence was found that mandated 1928 Thompson guns without compensators were to be updated when brought in for service or repair.

20

A **motor-cycle** unit taking aim with " Tommy " guns
Un détachement de motocyclistes avec ses mitrailleuses "Tommy" en position
En motorsykkelavdeling tar sikte med ,,Tommy'' maskingeverer
Een motorrijwiel-afdeeling mikt met ,,Tommy''-geweren

ABOVE: A picture taken from the March 1941 issue of *Neptune* magazine showing a row of British soldiers on motorcycles holding TSMG's. Note the arrows indicating two TSMG's without compensators. Also note both vertical and horizontal fore grips in use.

RIGHT: A picture most likely taken during the same photo shoot. Again, note the first rider is holding a TSMG without a compensator. Compare the motorcycle number of the first rider, C4340252, to the second rider in the picture above.

The Seventh Order

Authorization to order 54,000 additional Thompson guns appears to have been given on October 18, 1940, via a telegram titled Suply 133 or Suply 139. The uncertainty of the exact date is because neither telegram is contained in the available documentation. The number 54,000 was referenced in the negotiations with AOC over cancelling compensators on existing Thompson orders, above - "If we do not cancel compensators will be supplied without charge on 54,000 guns." [89] A November 11th cable reported, "Supplier has now signed contract for 54,000 guns with compensators at dollars 120 each with no reduction if compensation [sic] are omitted." The B.P.C. were still following orders and negotiating a price reduction for omitting compensators - "We believe according to our contract we can still cancel compensators at dollars 16 cents 67 each on most of the 25,000 guns still due for 1940. We await your instructions. [90] As stated above, those instructions came on November 13th and the compensator issue was resolved.

A synopsis of the deal involving compensators and the new order for 54,000 more Thompson guns was set forth in another telegram on November 20th. "Since placing order A-2308 for 54,000 Thompson sub-machine guns at 120 dollars each and since informing Auto-Ordnance that compensators will be continued on existing orders, the company has given us a quotation, for further orders in lots of 25,000 guns or more, of 110 dollars per gun with compensator and spare parts at a discount of 50%." The telegram went on to state that AOC would probably increase their production to 12,000 guns per month by January 1941 and be able to complete deliveries on all orders by June 1941. [91] It appeared all the fuss over the cost of compensators resulted in the MoS obtaining their $110 price per gun on future orders. Moreover, all the guns would be equipped with compensators!

A New Scale for Ammunition and Submachine Guns

The submachine gun was well on its way to becoming standard equipment with the British military. On October 21, 1940, the Director of Staff Duties (Weapons) issued a memorandum discontinuing the temporary scale of ammunition issue for the Thompson gun and implementing a "full war establishment scale." The memorandum also set forth the War Office present intent to issue submachine guns on the following scale: [92]

Guns:
Infantry Battalion – 36 (1 per section in rifle companies)
Motor-cycle Battalions – 33 (1 per section in Scout and motor-cycle platoons)

Drums: (holding 50 rounds)
5 per gun on man*, 10 per gun in unit reserve

Magazines: (holding 20 rounds)
5 per gun on man, 20 per gun in unit reserve

---

[89] CYPHER TELEGRAM NEW YORK, 30th October 1940
[90] CYPHER TELEGRAM NEW YORK, 11th November 1940
[91] CYPHER TELEGRAM NEW YORK, 20th November 1940
[92] (WO199/3249) War Office Memorandum by D.S.D. (w) Daryl Hickes, dated 21st October, 1940
Author's Note: The Gale & Polden manual (Page 5), The Thompson Submachine Gun Mechanism Made Easy, shows a fully loaded 50 round Thompson drum weighs 4.75 pounds. A fully loaded 20 round magazine weighs 1.25 pounds.

The Last Colt Thompsons

One question that has never been answered is what happened to the remaining 100 Colt manufactured Thompson guns in AOC inventory after the Swedish government made the 500 Thompson gun purchase in January 1940. Why didn't AOC immediately ship these remaining 100 Colt guns to the British as part of their initial order? A partial answer to this question may be found in a letter from the British Purchasing Commission (B.P.C.) to the MoS, dated November 6th 1940. The letter tells about the British assumption of the (second) French contract F-53 (3000 guns) and a proposed shipment of "149 new guns and about 40 second-hand guns, the latter being thoroughly reconditioned in every way."

When France fell, the British assumed the French contract with AOC for Thompson guns. AOC agreed that it had not meet the delivery schedules in the contract negotiated by the French and about one-half (1500) of the guns remained undelivered. The penalty agreed to by AOC for not meeting the delivery schedule is "some 300 guns were to be furnished free of charge by the supplier." The 149 new guns and 40 reconditioned second hand guns appear to be a portion of this penalty. After the British negotiated the penalty, they cancelled the contract because the price negotiated by the French was higher than the current British price. This shipment would contain the 149 new guns and "29 of the second-hand guns." "The remaining 11 second-hand guns will follow shortly." [93] Of course, this begs for more information on the pedigree of the 40 second-hand or used Thompson guns referenced in this letter. It is very possible these used Thompson guns were the last Colt guns in AOC inventory. It is known AOC had 175 "Second Hand" guns in inventory on July 26, 1934. [94] These were most likely accumulated from testing, demonstrations, salesman samples, returns, etc. during the many years AOC spent marketing the Thompson submachine gun. It would also explain why AOC did not immediately ship the remaining 100 Thompson guns alleged to be in inventory to the British upon receipt of their first order.

A BPC spreadsheet of miscellaneous French contracts that were cancelled or amended, dated June 16, 1940, revealed the number of Thompson guns to be furnished "free or charge" to Britain was 150. Another stipulation denoted Auto-Ordnance was to return the balance of the French advance "to B.P.C. for account of French State." [95] No documentation was found that explained how initially 150 free Thompson guns later became 300 free guns that included 40 second-hand reconditioned guns.

The Eighth Order

On December 23rd 1940, R.J. Sinclair, D.G.A.R., penned a SECRET letter to G.W. Turner indicating the Treasury had approved "an additional order for 50,000 Thompson Sub-machine Guns." Sinclair stated that it was likely additional orders would be forthcoming as the supply of rifles was not sufficient although he did not believe the Thompson gun was preferable to the .30 caliber rifle. Of this new order, the Home Guard was asking for 40,000 of these Thompson guns to equip their forces. [96]

Sinclair told how he had learned that a new factory was being "laid out in America for the production of Thompson guns," but he did not believe this would result in an immediate increase in the supply of Thompson guns. He was of the opinion a quicker path to increased supply was to have the present production facility work longer hours with additionally provided machine tools. He also inquired

---

[93] Letter from W.E. Leigh, B.P.C., to MoS, dated November 6th, 1940
[94] Auto-Ordnance Corporation – Inventory of Assembled Salable Firearms, etc., dated July 26, 1934
[95] (AVIA 38/62) Miscellaneous French Contracts Assigned to B.P.C. at June 16, 1940 Canceled or Amended by B.P.C.
[96] Letter (SECRET) from Sinclair to Turner, dated December 23rd 1940

whether the production capacity of the Johnson self-loading rifle would help reduce the British shortage of rifles. [97]

Turner replied to Sinclair in a SECRET letter on December 28th attaching a copy of the telegram he sent to the Commission asking them to order 50,000 more Thompson guns. He requested Sinclair specify the number of magazines and amount of ammunition authorized with this order. He acknowledged Sinclair's desire to place an ever larger order of Thompson guns and said, "we shall be in a better position to judge the desirability of arranging that when we get a reply to the present cable." He also inquired if Sinclair wanted to pursue any other rifle besides the Johnson and suggested that they should submit an inquiry covering all alternative rifles of interest. However, in the meantime he agreed to check on the Johnson rifle. [98]

The order for these 50,000 Thompson guns also contained an assumption directed at AOC stating this order should allow production to increase to approximately 14,000 guns per month. Further information was requested from AOC on additional quantities and rates of delivery if the British took every Thompson gun produced until June 1942. [99]

On January 17, 1941, Munitions Production Central (M.P.C.) documented the complete order as 50,000 guns, 150,000 drum magazines, 250,000 box magazines, 100 million rounds of ammunition and spares in same proportion as ordered in the past. [100]

AOC quickly responded to inquiries about new orders versus increased production - "… production will be increased to 1,000 guns per diem [day] or approximately 23,000 per mensem [month] by May 1941 and that 71,460 undelivered on present orders as of 1st January will all be delivered by 1st June and 50,000 additional by 15th August. Price on these guns will not exceed 110 including compensations [sic]." AOC went on to state that would leave a capacity of 100,000 guns, which have not been contracted for. The British were somewhat skeptical of AOC proposed production numbers but agreed production had been increasing and that the 100,000 gun unordered capacity could be delivered by March 1942. Of special note was the following statement by AOC, "Supplier insists on keeping small part of his capacity for U.S. Government and other small orders largely from law – enforcing bodies."*[101] The telegram concludes with information the Reising gun is going to be placed into production in February (1941) but no report on the test gun supplied on November 5th has been received. The Reising gun "shoots .45 calibre pistol ammunition and is priced at under $50." There is also a brief reference to a gun by "high standard" supplied for testing. [102]

Turner sent a follow up letter to Sinclair on January 9, 1941, stating the B.P.C. order for 50,000 more Thompson guns "has greatly improved delivery prospects, and that the supplier expects that production will reach 23,000 per month by next May." Turner added that the Commission considered the suppliers delivery predictions as "optimistic," but believes that production would increase. He asked Sinclair for his views on placing additional orders of the Thompson gun to utilize all of AOC's future production

---

[97] *Ibid*
[98] Letter (SECRET) from Turner to Sinclair, dated December 28rd 1940
[99] CYPHER TELEGRAM NEW YORK, SUPLY 1274, 28th December 1940
[100] Immediate War Orders, Thompson Sub machine Guns…[218/9], signed by G.W. Turner, P.A.S.(P.), dated Jan 17, 1941
Author's Note: Thompson guns manufactured by Savage Arms for AOC and sold to law enforcement organizations in the USA by AOC are commonly referred to by collectors in America as "Savage Commercial Thompsons." This is a collector term and not an official AOC designation or variation. This statement is the first seen by the author that recognizes AOC acknowledged or was even interested in making these types of small sales.
[101] CYPHER TELEGRAM NEW YORK, 4th January 1941
[102] *Ibid*

capacity. Turner ended the letter by stating the two weapons in question by Sinclair earlier (the Reising and High Standard), "are in the design stage only, and could not be accepted as service weapons." [103]

All the past negativity surrounding the Thompson gun was changing. No longer just a weapon for the Irish Republican Army or American gangsters, this submachine gun from America was fast becoming a part of the culture for younger generations. (Hobbies Weekly, November 16th, 1940)

_____

[103] Letter (SECRET) from Turner to Sinclair, dated 9th January 1941

Production Issues

The MoS was aware that future production capabilities set forth by AOC always appeared on the high end – especially when trying to garner a new order. Nevertheless, these production goals and projections were serious business to the MoS. On January 6th 1941, G.W. Turner requested an explanation, "to the delivery position of Thompson M/G. i.e. Oct. 700; Nov. 9644; Dec. 4849 (7550) *in transit* [handwritten comment] in relation to the cable dated 14/10/40 which promised deliveries of 8,000 for October increasing to 12/14,000 by January 1941, and to request you take further action to ascertain the latest production *"& delivery"* [handwritten comment] position for forecast purposes." [104] In other words, why was AOC not meeting its stated projections?

The reply from R. Cullen, MoS, stated deliveries or shipments "have fallen short of the promise of the 14/10/40 cable if it is assumed that the rise to 12/14000 per month by January is a gradual one. Ex factory deliveries (shipments) from the factory have been Oct 5010, Nov 8128, Dec 8105." The answer continued with the promise in an earlier cable of a production rate of 23,000 per month by May 1941. [105] The B.P.C. responded with a January 11th cable that estimated Thompson gun deliveries as January – 10,000, February – 12,000, March – 14,000, April – 16,000 and May – 20,000. [106] The 14/10/40 cable referenced several times in the above correspondence was not located.

How Many Thompson Guns?

A SECRET letter from Col. L.F.S. Dawes of the War Office, North American Bureau, to G.W. Turner dated January 10, 1941, titled, "Extra Thompson Guns," demonstrated perfectly how the exact number of Thompson guns on order at any given time in the USA was most likely never really known by everyone in the process. Dawes, referring to the December 1940 order (eighth order) of 50,000 Thompson guns, stated the order was for 54,000 Thompson guns. Someone on the receiving end of the letter caught the mistake and wrote the number 50,000 below the number 54,000. The purpose of the letter was to direct inquires for what weapons, including rifles, the British can get "off the peg" with the proviso that ammunition is available. Dawes specifically referenced the past enquiry by Turner regarding the Johnson rifle. He also stated he would get financial sanction for whatever armaments Turner found that met British requirements. [107]

Dawes was not the only one confused with the British orders of Thompson guns. The MoS ledger books, already 750 guns in error, was about to make an even bigger mistake. As stated above, the total number of guns from British orders one through four was 55,250. The MoS ledger book showed 56,000 guns because someone had double counted the initial order of 750 guns. The fifth order of 17,000 guns and sixth order of 27,000 guns were added to the ledger book making the total number an even 100,000 guns. The next entry was for 50,000 guns, the eighth order. The seventh order for 54,000 guns was not recorded in the ledger book. [108]

Dawes was very busy in January 1941. In a SECRET letter to R. Cullen at the MoS, he referenced a telephone conversation regarding a "half million Thompson Guns." He stated the half million includes "110,000 ordered originally plus the 50,000 now ordered i.e., a balance of 340,000." Apparently, Cullen

---

[104] Minute Sheet No. 163A, dated January 6th 1941
[105] *Ibid*
[106] Cypher Telegram from the B.P.C., dated 11th January 1941
[107] Letter (SECRET) from Dawes to Turner, titled Extra Thompson Guns, dated 10th January 1941
[108] Ministry of Supply, SUPP 4-310 – Contract Record Books: THOMPSON SUB-MACHINE GUNS

took issue with the figure of 110,000 guns on order and made a handwritten note the number should be 108,000 according to the U.S.A. programming tables and contract history sheets; the balance from 500,000 is actually 342,000. [109]

from the Bill & Carol Troy collection, USA

Undated newspaper photograph titled, "Training our Paratroops." British paratroops, prepared for their skilled and daring work by the Army and Royal Air Force are a volunteer force, whose training begins at a R.A.F. station. This is the type of man that is in our Parachute Corps – armed with a Tommy Gun.

54,000…or 50,000?

With all the uncertainty concerning the order for 54,000 Thompson guns in October 1940 and another order for 50,000 Thompson guns in January 1941, the question arises if this was just one order and everyone was confused. Alternatively, were there actually two orders of slightly different amounts - and everyone was confused? Jumping ahead slightly for the immediate sake of clarity, the question was finally resolved in a March 11, 1941, Cypher Telegram from the Consul General in New York - "He

---

[109] Letter (SECRET) from Dawes to Cullen, dated 11th January 1941

[Auto-Ordnance] estimates he will complete our A-2304 calling for 54,000 guns in early May and will then start on 50,000 we have pending on contract awaiting Washington financial release." [110] AOC and the B.P.C. knew exactly how many Thompson guns were on order. The "awaiting Washington financial release" stipulation is directly related to the new Lend-Lease Act of March 11, 1941, the same day as the Cypher Telegram.

A review of all known documentation offers no explanation why the officials at the MoS who were maintaining the ledger books of goods ordered for the war effort were not aware of both orders. A required "Initial War Orders" memorandum, later changed to "Immediate War Orders" (IWO) for "Thompson Sub machine Guns, magazines, ammunition and spares" issued by the Munitions Production Central (M.P.C.) detailing the 54,000 Thompson gun order was never issued. However, this IWO memorandum was issued for the 50,000 Thompson gun order on January 17th 1941 (and with all previous orders) and cited in the MoS ledger book. [111] The M.P.C. IWO issue sequence of the 50,000 gun order - 218/9 - followed in sequence the previous order of 27,000 Thompson guns - 218/8.

It is unknown how Dawes reached the 110,000 total he referenced in the January 11, 1941 letter to Cullen cited above. However, a handwritten table titled. **"PRE LEASE LEND REQUIREMENTS"** attached to the inside cover of the MoS folder used as the primary basis of this story may explain how Cullen at the MoS reached the 108,000 figure. The table lists the initial order of 750 guns, a 55,250 gun order (the combined total of the 2,000 gun order, the two orders of 26,250 guns, and the mistake of double counting the initial order of 750 guns for a total of 55,250), the 17,000 gun order, the 27,000 gun order and the 50,000 gun order. This perfectly matches the figures found in the MoS ledger book as 150,000 Thompson guns on order. However, there is an asterisk beside the 50,000 gun order that stated, "42,000 of this order now under L.L." or Lend-Lease. If you subtract these 42,000 guns noted as being supplied under Lend-Lease from the 150,000 gun total, 108,000 Thompson guns matches Cullen's figure, above. A copy of this table can be found toward the end of the story (p. 100). Irrespective of Dawes, Cullen, the table, or the MoS ledger book, there is no accounting for the 54,000 Thompson gun order or contract A-2304. Despite all discrepancies, Dawes instructed Cullen to find out how many Thompson guns could be delivered by April 1942 in addition to the 50,000 in the eighth order if a "colossal order" of Thompson guns were made. Dawes was careful to state this was only an enquiry, not a firm order for more guns. [112]

The (initial) Ninth Order: How Many MORE Thompson Guns?

Apparently the 108,000 figure cited by Cullen took hold as a January 14, 1941, telegram stated - "The total number of Thompson Guns which you have ordered in the U.S.A., inclusive of the 50,000 authorized in our SUPLY 1274, is 158,000." Of course, this did not explain that 8,000 Thompson guns in this 108,000 gun total were actually received under the 50,000 gun order (and the balance of 42,000 guns would be procured under Lend-Lease). Inaccuracies with the procurement numbers for the Thompson gun were now the norm - but it did allow all parties to use the same numbers.

The telegram went on to state that because of the 50,000 gun order there should be an increase in monthly deliveries by May of 1941. The question then became how much more capacity would be available with additional orders. "If a decision were reached to order more Thompson Guns, time would

---

[110] CYPHER TELEGRAM NEW YORK, 11th March 1941

[111] Immediate War Orders, Thompson Sub machine Guns, magazines, ammunition and spares [218/9] signed G.W. Turner, P.A.S.(P.), dated January 17, 1941 and Ministry of Supply, SUPP 4-310 – Contract Record Books

[112] Letter (SECRET) from Dawes to Cullen, dated 11th January 1941

be the governing factor, and our requirements might be defined as the greatest possible number of Thompson Guns within a maximum of 500,000 including orders already placed to date which could be delivered by April, 1942." The telegram plainly stated no decision on future orders have been made but the "decision will be largely determined by the prospects of increased production." [113] While British officials were debating on acquiring more Thompson guns, a message to the D.G.A.R. revealed that "…until the President of the U.S.A. has settled procedure on his policy of assistance to Great Britain, contractors will not act on further orders." [114] An undated telegram or message that was a "Further to our [SUPLY] 1274 of 29 December…" believed to have been authored in mid- January 1941 stated - "We now require a further 100,000 of these guns for delivery beginning on completion of present order." This instruction was given as a requirement with the understanding under "present circumstances" it is not possible to place actual order but to do so "as soon as possible." [115]

The MoS was not sitting idle during this time when orders were frozen. Robert Burns at the MoS made a handwritten notation on an internal document, Minute Sheet No. 5, that indicated that the MoS has been unable to place the earlier 50,000 gun order but "there may be some advantage to having all our firm demands ready when the dam breaks." [116] And the dam would soon break with the British hungry for more Thompson guns. On January 23rd an order was given to order 100,000 additional Thompson guns with the following instructions - "In negotiating with the firm this prospect of a further order may prove the means of inducing manufacturer to expand capacity in a manner which will be reflected also on current orders." [117]

The response from the Consul General in New York for how much increased production could be expected with another large order came on January 24, 1941 - the day after a decision was made to place a large order! AOC advised that they believe they can deliver 66,000 guns in the next four months beginning February 1st. They then believe they can deliver 152,000 guns in the fifth through eighth months and 188,000 in the ninth through twelfth months for a total of 406,000 guns. All of this was predicated on AOC being able to obtain the necessary "machine tool equipment." Price was not discussed but it was believed the price would not go much lower than the current $110 price per gun. The Consul General cautioned the above figures were optimistic but believed the production totals "could be met by end of April 1942 however if orders were placed at once." [118] How fast things can change in war. Almost one year after ordering the first 750 guns, Great Britain was all in with the Thompson Gun.

The Précis

An undated précis (pronounced "pray-see") or summary document titled, "Ammunition for Sub Machine Guns .45 and 9 mm," authored in or around January 1941 summed up the Thompson gun in Great Britain perfectly:

1. 100,000 Thompsons will have been delivered by June 1941 (Suply 719).
2. Schmeisser Gun production will be under way about June 1941.
3. Smith & Wessons (20,000 or alternatives) will not have been delivered before June 1941.

---

[113] TELEGRAM NEW YORK, Thompson Guns, SUPLY 282, 14th January 1941
[114] COPY of message or minutes to D.G.A.R., 177A, dated January 16, 1941
[115] Undated message or telegram, notation of 177B on top right hand corner.
[116] Handwritten notation on Minute Sheet No. 5 (180) by Robert Burns, MoS, dated January 20, 1941
[117] TELEGRAM NEW YORK, Thompson Guns, 23 January 1941
[118] CYPHER TELEGRAM NEW YORK, 24TH January 1941

Continuing, by the end of February 175 million rounds of .45 caliber (131 million) and 9mm caliber (44 million) would have been delivered. A balance of 272 million rounds was still on order and expected to be delivered at a rate of "21 million a month" by the end of March 1942. Regarding Thompsons, the précis revealed, "That further orders for Thompson may be expected in view of fact that these guns are at present our only certainty and therefore most likely to be available to meet pressing demands from Home Guard, Dominions and Allies. Further orders will involve further .45 ammunition." [119]

The American Gangsters

The mass quantities of war equipment shipped to Great Britain did not escape the attention of the criminal element in America. The shipyards in New York and other places were filled with a variety of goods that were very valuable on the black market. The Thompson gun certainly fit this category. On February 22, 1941, according to the *New York Times*, "a wooden case containing ten Thompson submachine guns destined for the British Army" disappeared from Pier 54, "a heavily guarded Cunard Line pier on the Hudson River." New York City detectives and agents from the Federal Bureau of Investigation (FBI) responded to the crime scene. The packing case, "three feet long by two feet wide and weighing 150 pounds, was one of 102 cases of submachine guns delivered to the pier" from the "Auto-Ordnance Company of Utica, New York." The cases were stacked on the pier, "awaiting shipment of the British motorship Silver Cedar."

A police marine squad was summoned to look for the packing case and guns in the water. The FBI became involved on the basis that the theft might have been the work of "anti-British forces." Grappling operations by the police marine squad had recovered sections of the wooden packing case; this seemed to bolster the sabotage theory by anti-British agents. The paper revealed, "Each case contained complete parts for the guns, including butt stocks, cleaning rods, brass brushes, magazines, and ten handbooks giving instructions for assembling and using the weapons. They had been bought by the British Purchasing Commission, the police said." Of note, "500 or more cases of ammunition and other materials for Britain" was also on the pier awaiting shipment. [120]

An anonymous telephone call to New York City Detective James Argenza resulted in the recovery of the ten weapons the next day. All ten guns were found in "three burlap sacks tied with twine" in a vacant lot behind Tony's Barber Shop on West Fifteenth Street, a location close to the pier. The tip and subsequent discovery of the weapons lead the police to believe the theft was not the work of anti-British forces or gangsters but an ordinary theft by local criminals who "...probably got cold feet." The guns were described as completely assembled, barrels clean, packing oil removed and not damaged. They were photographed, fingerprinted, and taken "to the West Twentieth Street Station, where they will be held until the owners claim them." The packing case with the exception of the top cover was recovered from the waters at the foot of Pier 54. [121]

The motorship Silver Cedar (correct name: *Silvercedar)* would survive this voyage, but her luck ran out on 15th October 1941 when she fell victim to a U-Boat S-E of Greenland. [122]

---

[119] Précis A.R.2 B.M. 3/15, 196A, undated but in January 1941 time frame
[120] "10 Guns for British Vanish From Pier Here; Fragments Indicate Box Might Be in River," *New York Times*, Feb. 22, 1941
[121] "TEN BRITISH GUNS FOUND IN LOT HERE," *New York Times*, February 23, 1941
[122] See Chapter Eight - The U-Boats! (p.96)

The Lend-Lease Act – March 11, 1941

Lend-Lease was the program under which the United States provided aid to Great Britain and other allies from March 11, 1941, until 1945. The enactment of the Lend-Lease Act had a definite impact on all pending orders of war material by Great Britain, including the Thompson gun. As stated above, the March 11, 1941, Cypher Telegram that solved the mystery of the 54,000 and 50,000 Thompson gun orders specifically referenced "waiting Washington financial release" as related to the start of the last 50,000 gun order. The telegram went on to state that another order of 100,000 Thompson guns (the initial ninth order) was being held "in abeyance pending the Lend-lease Bill." "Next step depends on Lend-lease Bill and your and U.S. policy thereafter. Please advise if you want additional capacity developed. Ammunition production for these guns will have to be simultaneously increased." [123] The British policy of "cash and carry" was ending; Lend-Lease was the new law of the land.

from The American Thompson Reference Collection, USA

A February 20, 1941 newspaper photograph titled, "Canada's Western Ontario Regiment Trains In England." The description states that veteran Canadian soldiers, including many Americans volunteers, have joined up to help Britain with the war. Pictured are Major McDonald (left) and Lieut. C.P. Keeley taking cover during training - somewhere in England. Passed by Censors

---

[123] CYPHER TELEGRAM NEW YORK, 11th March 1941

What are your requirements?

A three page SECRET letter from G.W. Turner to Colonel L.F.S. Dawes, War Office, North American Bureau, on March 14, 1941, set in motion a discussion for increasing orders for the Thompson gun and requested the need "to know your definite requirements." A recap was made of the first six Thompson gun orders setting forth the numbers exactly as outlined in this story. It is interesting how the these six orders stated by the Principal Assistant Secretary (Production) of the MoS in this letter add up to 99,250 guns, yet his own ledger books indicate 100,000 Thompson guns. The "piecemeal ordering" along with the order of 50,000 guns was discussed. There was no direct reference to the previous order of 54,000 Thompson guns. The current need for the Thompson gun was because of the lack of rifles. The discussion then turned to totals and deliveries:

> "Your total orders then are 235,000, and there is another 17,000 for India and the Air Ministry. The order for the last 100,000 was held up until the Lend-Lease legislation should be in force, and the total quantity actually ordered is 99,340. There have been 37,383 delivered here or abroad and 6,788 are in transit, a total of 44,171. The promised deliveries are 14,000 in March, 16,000 April, 20,000 May, 23,000 June and onwards. At a conservative estimate you should be sure of your existing demands being met by March, 1942."

It is unknown what orders or documents were used by Turner to obtain the 235,000 figure cited above. Turner discussed briefly the Smith & Wesson, Schmeisser and STEN guns and ended with asking Dawes "to get settled firmly what your total requirements are to be." Five hundred thousand Thompson guns was stated to be the number each party had been using in the past to discuss requirements, but it was understood that this number was not approved. Turner believed a decision had to be made soon so the Americans could be told of the "offer of increased capacity which we have obtained from the Thompson Company, and invite them under the Lease-Lend arrangements to consider favourably undertaking this expansion." He ended by saying we have to bear in mind, "the Americans may be taking some of the output themselves." [124]

The last sentence of Turner's letter about the Americans "taking" some of the delivery of Thompson guns is very revealing. It is unknown what British officials knew about other AOC customers. The French, Canadians and Americans were obvious AOC customers or potential customers. It is also unknown what the Americans knew about the early British orders or any of the initial AOC clients. There is no reason to doubt Turner's delivery figures of 44,171 guns, cited above. The date these figures were recorded is unknown. Since March 1941 delivery projections were also cited in the letter, a strong inference could be formed these figures are for some time in February 1941 - or before. What is known are the Savage production figures for Thompson guns at the end of February 1941: 66,101 guns. Also known are the number of Thompson guns ordered by the U.S. Government for the year 1940 through February 1941: 20,454 guns though December 30, 1940 with another order of 10,626 guns on February 7, 1941. [125]

Adding Turner's figure of 44,171 guns in transit and delivered with U.S. Government contract orders of 20,454 Thompson guns through the end of January 1941 puts the total at 64,625 guns. Subtracting the 64,625 guns from the Savage production figure of 66,101 guns at the end of February leaves only 1476 guns to account for. Subtracting the 1150 guns originally sold to the French leaves only 326 unaccounted guns. Enter the Canadians. The Canadian government made three orders for Thompson

---

[124] SECRET Letter by Turner to Dawes, dated 14th March 1941
[125] Iannamico, 164-166, 169

guns and spare parts in June and July 1940: June 1940: 16 guns, July 4, 1940: 200 guns and July 18, 1940: 50 guns. [126] Subtract these 266 guns and the balance of unaccounted Thompson guns is down to 60, most or all of which can easily be attributed to sales to American law enforcement agencies. Simple analysis indicates for every 3 guns manufactured by Savage Arms for AOC, the British received two and the Americans received one. Russell Maguire's AOC was scrambling to keep everyone happy!

CANADIAN MILITARY HEADQUARTERS,

2, COCKSPUR STREET,

TRAFALGAR SQUARE,

LONDON, S.W.1.

The Canadians

The initial 266 Thompson guns obtained by the Canadian military in 1940 must have been well received. It appears the Canadian military may have started serious negotiations with AOC for larger quantities of Thompson guns in early 1941. The Director General of Munitions Production, MoS, received a letter dated 10 Mar 41 from Canadian Military Headquarters requesting price information for the Thompson gun and accessories. [127] Obviously, the Canadians did not want to pay more for the Thompson guns than the British! On March 21st the following information was provided to the Canadian military: [128] (*based on the British pound Sterling of twelve pennies = one shilling, twenty shillings = £1*)

Gun excluding spares	£27.10.0 each *[twenty-seven pounds, ten shillings]*
Drum magazine	1.10.0 each
Box magazine	7.0 each
Ammunition	5.12.0 per 1000 rounds

The Chicago Buccaneers order 25,000 additional guns!

The majority of the Cypher Telegrams found prior to the passage of the Lend-Lease Act were from the Consul General in New York and the B.P.C. A new name in the Thompson documentation appeared on March 29, 1941: Military Mission Washington. Their first Cypher Telegram in the documentation was designated Milmi 69 and it referenced a telephone conversation, 25,000 more Thompson guns and some mortars. [129]

Civil servants following government regulations engaged in acquiring property for any government endeavor have a thankless job. Compound that with your country being in a world war whose outcome is uncertain, these "bean counters," as they are often known, have to have a great sense of humor – just to survive. In the military it is always best to stay on the good side of those that supply your pay, rations and ammo, and not necessarily in that order. When procedures go astray, the conversation can get interesting. Robert Burns of the MoS had most likely seen one too many policy violations from the War

[126] Iannamico, 110, 111
[127] Letter from Canadian Military Headquarters to MoS, dated 10 Mar 41
[128] Letter to Canadian Military Headquarters, dated 21st March, 1941
[129] Cypher Telegram To the Military Mission Washington, dated 29th March 1941

Office when MILMI 69 crossed his desk. His subsequent internal report fits perfectly with the rousing history of the American gangster gun:

> It has always been a source of comfort to me that I had the War Office at my back to keep me straight in placing orders in North America. They have been very restrained in their demands and the soul of propriety. This feeling of comfort has lately been replaced by the eager anticipation of a life of luxurious sloth when the War Office once more took upon themselves the sordid commercial business of supply, which they were so glad to rid themselves of only two years ago. That millennium seems to have arrived. You will not have forgotten our passage of arms, the struggles of a dying age, on the subject of Vickers Belts, a small matter but significant. When the War Office come to deal with Tommy guns the spirit of the Chicago buccaneers seems to have entered into them. You know we have outstanding a cable asking us for a firm statement of our future demands for these guns and you know that the War Office, following after false gods, have decided to forsake the Tommy guns and go for Stens. On the other hand, the blandishments of their mission has persuaded them to offer a sop in the shape of an order for an extra 25,000 guns, accompanied by ammunition, and they have been so eager to offer this appeasement that they have not felt it necessary to go through the formality of consulting us. No doubt they felt that such a modest increase on our order did not justify breaking in on our slumbers.

> I saw MILMI 69, which I attach, yesterday evening and spoke to Major Laws, who told me that D.G.A.R. had sent the telegram and told A.R.2 that they ought to consult the MoS – and so they meant to, worthy fellows, but the telegram was already being cyphered by S.S.4.C. They had already told the commission to go ahead on this basis and, as the producer and presumably the B.P.C. are anxiously awaiting news of our further order, we can but assume that they will set upon the official intimation. I told Major Laws, therefore that I would let his telegram go but that I was sure that it would be frowned on here and that if the damage had not already been done I should have been forced to suspend action until I could consult higher authority.

> MILMI 65, which I also attach shows that the War Office are not completely beyond the pale and do occasionally recognize that we have an interest in a telegram but I am convinced that we shall never get satisfactory arrangements until a protest is made on the highest level. Incidentally, how we are to square the Treasury on Thompson guns I do not know. I hope you will agree to take this up vigorously with the D.G.A.R.

That this internal correspondence regarding the procurement of the Thompson gun survived is a testament to British record keeping. Mr. Burns' superior, G.W. Turner, simply acknowledged Mr. Burns concerns by writing "Seen" with his initials and date, March 31, 1941. [130]

Unfortunately, what conversations took place between the MoS and the War Office because of Burns' dissertation are not detailed in the documentation. And nothing would be gained by creating a record of that conversation for posterity. However, a telegram marked "not sent" references the MILMI 69 Cypher Telegram and stated, "It is confirmed that you should order a further 25,000 Thompson Sub-Machine Guns with ammunition on the scale of 2,000 rounds per gun." "This order confirms the order in MILMI 69." The unsent telegram says "we" would like to see increased production of the Thompson so we could get our existing orders sooner but realize that may not be possible without "greatly increased orders." [131] Perhaps, what Mr. Burns started had something to do with this telegram not being sent, at

---

[130] Typed statement from Robert Burns, MoS, on Minute Sheet paper (233), to P.A.S.(P.), dated .3.41
[131] "Not Sent" Telegram referencing MILMI 69, undated

least not immediately. Burns penned another message to the P.A.S.(P.) stating, "We have no official letter from the War Office asking us to order a further 25,000 Thompson Guns, but I think we ought to follow up MILMI 69 with a telegram confirming the order and adding to it the Magazines and Spares which the War Office have overlooked." [132]

Review of all available documentation indicates Robert Burns was a major player at the MoS with the procurement of Thompson guns. While he continued his push to order the above referenced 25,000 Thompson guns, he provided this perspective to his superior:

I understand from the War Office that this is the sum of their further demands for Thompsons. As you know, they have asked us for a further 142,000 Sten Guns, although I am not sure that they have done so in a formal letter. I am firmly convinced that we shall have a further demand for Thompsons before Summer. They have decided to go for Stens under the impression that they have a good chance of getting 100,000 of them by the end of the year. I do not believe they will, and I think, when they discover this, they will put in another demand for Thompsons as a stop-gap. I think it will then be very difficult to persuade the producers to increase the capacity to the necessary extent. [133]

Robert Burns knew the British military would not be denied another 25,000 Tommy guns because someone in the War Office did not know how to follow procedures. A Cypher Telegram on April 3rd, 1941, from the Military Mission Washington stated the "Expenditure program under LL covers 400,000 Thompson sub machine guns by June 42 the 25,000 for Allies would have to come out of this or from deliveries to U.S. Army." It also references but does not explain something called the 'B' program. [134] A draft telegram to New York with a handwritten cypher date of April 9th references a telephone conversation with G.W. Turner in which the "Thompson Gun Programme" was shown at 500,000 guns. However, the current commitments were as follows, "These were 258,000 plus 6,000 for Programme B. plus a further 25,000 erroneously notified by the War Office by telephone and in Milmi 69 and now definite. Total 289,000." Turner goes on to state the reason for the current limitations "include reactions on rifle and ammunition programmes and possibilities of production of Sten pattern here. Ammunition supply not easy." Then he shows himself and his staff committed to obtaining whatever is needed for the war effort by ending the telegram with the following, "On the other hand if you are committed beyond this figure we do not desire you to retreat but to advise us of position early." [135] The number of Thompson guns awaiting contract approval and manufacturing authorization because of the Lend-Lease Act had just increased by 25,000 because of a telephone call and 6,000 for Programme B (a program designed to provide Great Britain with 10 military divisions worth of U.S. Pattern equipment). The firm number of Thompson guns needed was now at 289,000.

Thompson orders under the Lend-Lease Act

The passage of the Lend-Lease Act insured that Great Britain would acquire all the war material necessary to fight a war against the Axis forces. However, from a bureaucratic standpoint it changed the rules of the procurement game. The obvious discrepancies in the number of Thompson guns ordered or on order cited in official documents continued unabated. By March 1941, AOC had not delivered all the

---

[132] Typed statement from Robert Burns, MoS, on Minute Sheet paper (235), to P.A.S.(P.), dated April 2, 1941
[133] Ibid
[134] Cypher Telegram From the Military Mission Washington, dated 3rd April 1941
[135] Draft Telegram to New York from Turner, dated (handwritten) April 9, 1941; telegram approved by the Treasury and dispatched, E.G. Penman, MoS, same date, handwritten Minute Sheet (237)

Thompson guns contracted for under cash and carry. The total number of Thompson guns manufactured by Savage Arms for AOC at the end of March 1941 was 84,780 - and not all the production was going to Great Britain. [136] Most likely, perfect numbers were not as important as continued shipments of Thompson guns.

On April 12, 1941, a Cypher Telegram from the Military Mission Washington indicated that "…included in the first expenditure programme 400,000 Thompson sub machine guns for delivery by June 42." However, it went on to say that the MoS has since reduced the requirement to "about 200,000" and wanted confirmation that this was agreed to because of the pending rifle shortage. [137]

The response came quickly in another Cypher Telegram dated April 15, 1941, that stated when Lend-Lease went into effect the British contracts for Thompson guns totaled 108,000. Thompson gun requirements not contracted for are listed as "a) 150,000, b) 8,000 (_another new figure; it is possible this is a mistake and should have been 6,000_), c) 25,000 total 183,000." The telegram recounted the previous assurance of being prepared to accept up to 500,000 Thompson guns and cited this declaration as the basis why the negotiation under Lend-Lease was for an additional 400,000 more Thompson guns. The reason for the large requirement was the "known rifle shortage and strong possibilities of delays in production of rifles in America." For these reasons, "we hesitate finally to reduce our demand on U.S. to below 400,000." But in an effort to have it both ways, the telegram stated that the War Department was to be advised of a "possible downward revision" of Thompson guns. [138]

The decision as to the number of Thompson guns ultimately needed reached the highest levels of the British Military. An April 16th SECRET letter from R.J. Sinclair, D.G.A.R., to Vice-Admiral Harold Brown, D.G.M.P., discussed at length the Sten gun production and shortage of rifles. Sinclair agreed that another 25,000 Thompson guns were needed making the total "283,000 Thompson gun in all exclusive of Programme 'B')." He was very frank in stating the British preferred the Sten to the Thompson but realized the Thompson gun was in production and more Thompsons could be purchased over the 283,000 total if necessary. He was counting on the proposed production of the Sten to offset the need for additional Thompson guns. [139]

A response from Brown on April 18th indicated that he was looking into the "production possibilities of the Sten gun" but until the actual production began it was "extremely difficult to give reliable forecasts." Instead of just asking Sinclair to increase the order of Thompson guns via Lend-Lease, Brown went into a long description of possible production difficulties that could ultimately reduce the number of Sten guns produced during the next year. He then asked if a reduced projection for the production of Sten guns "would lead you to increase the order for Thompson guns." He ended the letter by stating, "[G.W.] Turner has already explained to you the position in regard to orders for Thompson guns and the importance of settling now any further requirements we want to place." [140] Obviously, Brown wanted more Thompson guns but he would not unequivocally state that position.

A telegram to the B.P.C. on April 23rd attempted to put some order into the current needs of the Thompson gun - "Must emphatically point out that Suply 282 of 14th January made clear that 500,000 (five hundred thousand) was not a firm requirement." It further stated the firm requirement to date was 289,000 but another 25,000 was being added to this for a new firm gross requirement of 314,000

---

[136] Iannamico, 165
[137] Cypher Telegram From the Military Mission Washington, dated April 12th 1941
[138] Cypher Telegram From the Consul General in New York, dated April 15th 1941
[139] SECRET letter from R.J. Sinclair to Harold Brown, dated 16th April 41
[140] SECRET letter from Harold Brown to R.J. Sinclair, dated 18th April 41

Thompson guns. It also cautioned not to let the current orders to date plus Lend-Lease requisition exceed this number. [141]   With the new Sten gun not in production and rifles still in short supply, the Thompson gun procurement was unquestionably headed to 500,000. The new management team at AOC certainly believed new orders would be forthcoming. A new factory in Bridgeport, Connecticut, was only four months away from delivering the first 1928 Thompson. [142]

The B.P.C. responded on May 1st that "Formal requisition has now been made under Lease-Lend for 206,000 repeat 206,000 guns and 1,030,000 box magazines..." If 314,000 are the number of Thompson guns wanted and 108,000 have been ordered and/or are in the process of being shipped, that would leave a balance of 206,000. [143]

from the Illustrated London News, April 25, 1942
A drawing by Captain Bryan de Grineau, a "special artist" working for the Illustrated London News, depicting British soldiers engaged in a training exercise with live ammunition "Somewhere In England." Pictures and drawings of British soldiers with the Thompson gun in battle would be common during the war.

The Numbers...again

An undated handwritten document titled, "Scale of Magazines" that appeared to have been written in very late April or early May 1941 indicated someone tried to sort out the uncertainty of the procurement numbers that existed with the Thompson gun. This document listed the earlier Thompson gun orders by amount and listed the numbers of drums and box magazines associated with each order. The last entry initially appeared to be 25,000 guns but someone wrote the numbers 54 over the 25 to show 54,000

---

[141] Telegram to the B.P.C., dated April 23rd 1941
[142] Hill, 273-279, 323
[143] Cypher Telegram from the B.P.C., dated 1st May 1941

Thompson guns ordered. [144] Another handwritten document titled, "Memo," prepared in the same time frame reviewed the number of Thompson guns currently on order. The number 258,000 was shown based on the April 9, 1941, telegram cited above. Listed below the 258,000 figure were a "B Programme" order of 6,000 guns, a War Office telephone order of 25,000 guns that was ultimately accepted, and the most recent request for another 25,000 guns as requested in a telegram to the B.P.C. on April 23rd, referenced above. These four figures totaled 314,000 guns – the total number of Thompson guns requested to date. [145]

The handwritten document continued with listings of the "IWOs" or Immediate War Orders memorandums. The IWO for the first order of 750 guns, a penciled in IWO for the 2,000 gun second order, the third and fourth order of 55,250 guns (including the (cancelled) 2,000 gun second order and erroneously including the first 750 gun order). The fifth order of 17,000 guns (showing 12,000 to the Air Ministry and 5,000 to India), the sixth order of 27,000 guns and the 8th order of 50,000 guns. The (initial) ninth order of 100,000 guns was listed but with the notation, "No IWO issued." The total of these orders was 250,000 guns. There was no reference to the eighth order for 54,000 Thompson guns. At the bottom of the page is a handwritten message to Mr. Cullen of the MoS stating that a proposal is being made to issue a new IWO for 314,000 Thompson guns and cancel all the earlier IWOs. The author, whose signature is not legible, wants to know if Cullen would approve of this action. [146] The fact these two handwritten documents were created, saved and included in the documentation is a strong indication the problem with the procurement numbers were well known by those involved in the process.

On May 15, 1941, a decision not to accept additional 50 round drums, to attempt to cancel all pending drum orders, and to increase the order for box magazines was made. These actions are discussed later in the story. What is noteworthy about this decision is the back and forth banter about the number of box magazines that officials thought were on order and how many additional magazines were needed to fill the new projected requirements. Each official, one from the B.P.C. and one from the MoS, were attempting to explain to the other how they reached the numbers set forth in their respected telegrams. [147] Their discussions were very professional but the final response from Robert Burns, MoS, spoke volumes about the procurement process of the Thompson gun during the last 16 months - "As you know the figures for the various requirements connected with Thompson guns have always been open to some doubt. We have reached, however, some sort of finality on the basis of the 314,000 guns ordered and we have sent a cable Suply (   ) [Suply number is blank in source document] stating our firm requirement and giving you demand numbers. I do not think we should hesitate to exchange these explanatory telegrams on doubtful points." [148] Yes, the procurement of the Thompson gun was an ongoing nightmare concerning the accuracy of bureaucratic paperwork. But officials from the B.P.C. and MoS well understood their success or failure would be judged solely on how many of these weapons were placed in the waiting hands of the British war machine.

The Ninth Order...revised

On June 9, 1941, an Immediate War Orders (IWO) memorandum for "Thompson Sub machine Guns, magazines, Ammunition and Spares" was issued for 158,000 guns (218/10). A.J. Manson signed it for

---

[144] Handwritten document, Scale of Magazines (252A), undated
[145] Handwritten Memo setting forth orders of Thompson guns with question to Mr. Cullen, undated.
[146] Ibid
[147] Cypher Telegram from the B.P.C., For Burns from Reid, dated 27 May 1941
[148] Extract of Reid letter from B.P.C. of 28 May 1941 and Mr. Burns from MoS suggested reply

the D.G.M.P. [149] The proposal to cancel all existing IWOs referenced earlier must not have been approved as this IWO was sequentially numbered 218/10. The B.P.C. was notified that "various demand numbers" were used in covering the procurement requests in the current IWO. [150] All known demand numbers and (proposed) orders were previously discussed, above. On the same date this IWO was issued for 158,000 Thompson guns, an "Amended Copy" of the IWO with a large red "SECRET" stamp was issued for a "Special order placed in U.S.A. (Programme B)" for 6,000 guns and 50,000 box magazines. [151] Programme B was listed as an additional "Special" order at the very end of the MoS ledger book detailing the procurement of the Thompson submachine gun. [152]

This picture needs no introduction. It must have been a source of pride and reassurance for civilians to see motorized soldiers from the 3rd Infantry Division with machine guns on patrol, especially in the early days of the war when invasion was on everyone's mind.

---

[149] Immediate War Orders, Thompson Sub machine Guns…[218/10], signed A.J. Manson, dated June 9, 1941
[150] Cypher Telegram to the B.P.C. regarding Demand numbers, dated 12th June 1941
[151] Amended Copy Immediate War Orders, Sub machine guns…[381/9 Special], signed A.J. Manson, dated June 9, 1941
[152] Ministry of Supply, SUPP 4-310 – Contract Record Books

URGENT!!!

Officials at the MoS well understood ordering guns and receiving guns were not one in the same. The next month a telegram sent to the B.P.C. stressed the "urgent necessity of additional supplies of personal weapons here." The need for rifles was paramount as was the production of sub-machine guns in Britain. Further, "…it is of equal importance that delivery of Thompson guns, also their spares and ammunition, should be accelerated in any way possible. The same applies to pistols. The reasons for this are known to you." The goal was to place "every possible personal weapon in the hands of troops including the R.A.F. [Royal Air Force] and R.N. [Royal Navy] at the very earliest date possible." The Ministry wanted to know if the present forecast of 20,000 Thompsons a month "after Chinese requirements have been met can be improved on." [153]

There is never enough good news during a time of war – but it does come. A telegram from the B.P.C. on July 11th probably found wide circulation at the MoS - "The U.S. Ordnance Dept. informs us that by September of this year the total repeat total production of Thompson Sub-machine guns will amount to 50,000 a month." The Ordnance Dept. believed after allowing for the allocations for the U.S. and Chinese, the 206,000 Thompson guns requested under Lend-Lease would be completed by the end of 1942. The telegram ended with the B.PC. affirming they are in talks with U.S. officials on "how best to increase considerably the production of .45 calibre ammunition." [154] The projected increase in Thompson production coincided perfectly with the opening of the new AOC factory in Bridgeport, Connecticut in August 1941.

The first of many Lend-Lease Thompson guns

More good news was received on July 23, 1941. 30,000 Thompson submachine guns and approximately 150,000 box magazines were released to the B.P.C. under Lend-Lease. But there was more; the B.P.C. was further advised they could expect to "receive 6,000 Thompson guns per week thereafter." No information on the release of magazines was forthcoming but it was believed to be "in proportion of 5 magazines per gun." A number of these 30,000 guns and 150,000 box magazines were being used to fill diversion orders (sending British Thompson guns to destinations other than Great Britain). Of importance was the following statement, "Previously we were unable to send them because all the B.P.C. contracts had been completed. [155] Cash and carry for the Thompson gun was officially over.

Good news can change in an instant during wartime. A telegram from the B.P.C. on July 29, 1941, reduced the number of Thompson guns released to 20,000. However, the number of box magazines stayed the same. This caused some interruptions or delays in the diversion program. One diversion not delayed was the shipment of "86 guns with 2580 box magazines to M3 tank manufacturers to complete armament of first tanks coming off line under B.P.C. contracts." [156]

A New Rear Sight

The War Office and MoS were excellent stewards of the citizen's money. They had bargained and pushed to lower the price of each order with the new president of AOC, an experienced Wall Street financier who was used to having his way in negotiations. Their efforts in less than a year had lowered

---

[153] CYPHER TELEGRAM to the B.P.C. in WASHINGTON, 5th July 1941
[154] CYPHER TELEGRAM from B.P.C., WASHINGTON, 11th July 1941
[155] CYPHER TELEGRAM from B.P.C., WASHINGTON, 23rd July 1941
[156] CYPHER TELEGRAM from B.P.C., WASHINGTON, 29rd July 1941

the price of a new Thompson gun to $110 apiece. Now they were looking to save more money. On July 28th it was disclosed the Small Arms Committee was investigating the possibility of replacing the "unnecessarily complicated" Lyman rear sight with a "simple two range rock over aperture sight similar rifle number 4 mark one." The Lyman sight cost about five dollars; this new proposed rear sight would save approximately $3.00 per gun. The Small Arms Committee was flexible with a change to either a two-range rear sight or a fixed rear sight after testing. The design was complete for the two-range sight; it could be sent by air immediately. The design could also be changed to a fixed rear sight if so required. A request was made to begin negotiations with AOC and U.S. Ordnance for the introduction of a cheaper rear sight. The only concern was that the adoption of a new sight should not impact production.[157]

The response for a new and cheaper rear sight was fast - "One simple fixed sight for one hundred yards is accepted and can be introduced as soon as practical. Forward samples for schools and drawings." [158] While more cost cutting production measures for the Model 1928 Thompson gun would be implemented in the future, the first major modification appears to have been initiated by the MoS under Lend-Lease.

from the book "*TOMMY*" by Auto-Ordnance Vice-President Frederic A. Willis
An undated photograph from the new Auto-Ordnance factory at Bridgeport, Connecticut showing crates of newly manufactured Lend-Lease Thompson submachine guns being stacked for shipment overseas to allied forces. See below how many of these crates ended up in Great Britain. Auto-Ordnance literature provided the following weights and dimensions for the "specially designed strong boxes" used for shipment: Case containing ten guns - Dim. 36" x 12" x 15 1/2"; Net Weight 110 lbs; Gross 147 lbs.

[157] CYPHER TELEGRAM from B.P.C., WASHINGTON, 28th July 1941
[158] DRAFT CABLE, Suply 6850, 14th August 1941

Crates of Lend-Lease Thompson submachine guns from the Auto-Ordnance Corporation, United States of America, upon arrival at an ordnance depot in Great Britain, March 23, 1942.

The Tenth Order

The B.P.C. in a "Strictly confidential" telegram reported that they had been advised "in strict confidence by Savage Arms" that the U.S. Ordnance asked them what would be involved in changing from Thompson gun production to either automatic pistol or lightweight semi-automatic rifle. Savage reported that such a change would probably take six months but added they had enough Thompson orders for another 6 months of production. However, without additional future orders an impact could be felt in two months. The B.P.C. were of the opinion this would be the perfect time to place additional orders for the Thompson gun to keep the Savage production line in operation and also comply with the recent order stressing the need to procure all available personal weapons. [159] On July 30th an order was received to "requisition further 50,000 Thompson Sub-Machine Guns. Magazines and spares as

---

[159] CYPHER TELEGRAM from B.P.C., WASHINGTON, 30th July 1941

before."[160] The B.P.C. filed the requisition under Lend-Lease. [161] An IWO (218/11) for 50,000 guns was officially issued on August 12, 1941. [162] July 1941 was a busy month in the history of the Thompson gun.

A SECRET letter to Vice-Admiral Harold Brown, from D. Fisher, Deputy Director, Army Requirements, on July 29th told of this new order and stated the new total of Thompson guns was 358,000. It is unknown why the previously agreed Thompson procurement number of 314,000 (206,000 + 108,000) used to end all the confusion related to the procurement of the Thompson gun was simply ignored. Simple math indicates 314,000 total orders plus a new 50,000 order equals 364,000 Thompson guns. The letter also discussed the Sten requirements for Britain and Canada so it is possible this caused the confusion. [163] It is unknown if officials from the B.P.C. were made privy to the above letter but they responded on August 2, 1941 - "Total guns requisitioned before receipt of above cable 206,000." [164] The B.P.C. knew how many Thompson guns were ordered!

The Rifle Shortage Continues…Order More Thompson Guns!

The rifle shortage continued into the second half of 1941. The projected delivery of .303 caliber Lee-Enfield rifles from Savage Arms by the end of 1942 was projected to be approximately 400,000 rifles. The rate was expected to increase to 3000 a day when the Remington Ilion plant switched from production of .30 caliber rifles to .303 caliber rifles toward the end of 1942. There was concern about the less than expected output because the B.P.C. had requested over 500,000 .303 rifles and over 500,000 .30 caliber rifles. A push was on to find out what steps could be taken to increase production, especially at the Ilion plant in New York. The War Office made it perfectly clear to the B.P.C. that rifle production was a priority; the additional procurement of Thompson guns should be considered "partly stopgap to make good deficiency in rifles" production. [165]

The B.P.C. reported that the existing requisition of 206,000 Thompson guns and the additional requisition of 50,000 more would be completed "not later than February 1942." When these orders were completed, there might be a loss of production unless additional orders were received. The B.P.C. reported, "U.S. Ordnance Dept. would like to see an additional requisition placed for 500,000 Thompson sub machine guns which would occupy U.S. capacity during most of 1942." The B.P.C. requested that, "you place this demand on us" because of the great need for personal weapons and the current shortage of rifles even with the understanding that Thompson guns were "stop gap" armament. [166]

Stop gap or not, the British were now receiving a lot of these American submachine guns. And were about to receive even more. The genius of J. Russell Maguire to acquire a near defunct firearms company in 1939 with a 20-year-old stock of unsold weapons and to place that weapon back into production cannot be understated. While the investment looked brilliant in hindsight (and it was), the financial risk Maguire took was enormous.

As of September 7, 1941, 40,000 Thompson guns had been delivered to Great Britain under Lend-Lease.

[160] CYPHER TELEGRAM from B.P.C., WASHINGTON, 30th July 1941
[161] CYPHER TELEGRAM from B.P.C. WASHINGTON, 6th August 1941
[162] Immediate War Orders, Thompson Sub Machine Guns [218/11], signed A.J. Manson, dated August 12, 1941
[163] SECRET letter from D. Fisher, The War Office, to H. Brown, dated 29th July 1941
[164] CYPHER TELEGRAM from B.P.C. WASHINGTON, 2nd August 1941
[165] CYPHER TELEGRAM to the B.P.C., WASHINGTON, 28th August 1941
[166] CYPHER TELEGRAM from B.P.C. WASHINGTON, 31st August 1941

The shipment of these Lend-Lease guns were as follows: Tank Armament – 286, diversions or shipments from the USA to British interests and Dominions – 11,202, and directly to the United Kingdom – 28,512. Add this to the 108,000 Thompson guns purchased under cash & carry and it is easy to see how the Tommy gun was fast becoming a household name in Great Britain. Along with the guns, 374,216 box magazines had been provided to date (under Lend-Lease). At the end of September, less than three weeks away, another 50,000 guns and 75,000 magazines were scheduled to be released. This would be nearly 200,000 Thompson guns for British forces (108,000 + 40,000 + 50,000 = 198,000) with 3 months remaining in 1941. [167] The number of Thompson guns manufactured by Savage Arms and the newly opened AOC factory at the end of September 1941 was 221,001 guns. [168] The ratio of guns being delivered to the British had greatly increased since the enactment of Lend-Lease.

The B.P.C. asked permission to keep a store of 2000 guns and 10,000 magazines at a depot in the USA for immediate shipment for diversions. This would eliminate delay for future shipments of guns not going to the United Kingdom. [169]

The officials involved with the procurement of the necessary implements of war did display a sense of humor at times. A letter from R.C. Bryant at the MoS to L.F.S. Dawes of the North American Bureau of the War Office summed up several recent topics including how to "rouse our interest in the manufacture of the Sten in the United States" and a cable asking about the statistical reasons for a future immediate release of .30 caliber rifles - "By present standards both of these must now rank as chestnuts." [170]

from the book *"TOMMY"* by Auto-Ordnance Vice-President Frederic A. Willis
An undated photograph showing British soldiers guarding the "Libyan Coastal Frontier" with a Tommy gun at the ready.

---

[167] CYPHER TELEGRAM from B.P.C. WASHINGTON, 7th September 1941
[168] Iannamico, 165
[169] Ibid
[170] Letter from Bryant to Dawes, dated 9th September 1941

BRITAIN
AND HER
ALLIES ARE
RESOLVED
ON THIS ★ ★
that
come what may
the menace of
a world ruled
by force alone
shall be lifted
from the hearts
of men
by the strength
of those
who stand for
FREEDOM

THE BULL-DOG
BREED

Tens of thousands of guns of all types ; new, faster and more formidable tanks ; motorised guns, and dive-bombing aircraft for army co-operation continue to reach the British Armies as they prepare assiduously the counter-stroke against the Nazis.

Above : Men of a famous British regiment on field exercises with the deadly Thompson sub-machine guns.

Wt. 20239/P.1333. 7/41. F. & C. Ltd. 51-782

The front and back of a bookmark dated July 1941. The "deadly Thompson sub-machine guns" were fast becoming a part of British history.

The Eleventh Order

While it may have been tempting to order 500,000 more Thompson guns as per the U.S. Ordnance request, the next order was for 150,000 guns and 1,725,000 box magazines. There was a condition on this order; the guns and magazines must be delivered by June 1942. If this was not possible, the British would accept as many guns and magazines as could be manufactured up to this date. Of interest was no additional ammunition was being ordered. This order was deemed to be a stop gap measure because of the lack of personal weapons and current rifle deficiency. It was hoped, "This extra order, however, increases the desirability of accelerating deliveries of the ammunition already ordered." [171] The B.P.C. made the requisition but cautioned, "the actual quantity we shall receive by then depends on firstly our ability to provide financing from the new appropriation and secondly the allocation made to us by the

---

[171] Telegram, 8017 SUPLY, dated September 11, 1941

U.S. Government." [172] An IWO (218/12) for 150,000 Thompson guns and 1,725,000 box magazines was issued on September 25, 1941. One caveat of note - "Instructions on spares will follow." [173]

An undated telegram marked "WAIT" in capital letters referenced the September 11th SUPLY 8017 telegram ordering 150,000 Thompson guns, above, and requested, "requisition further 250,000 Thompson guns." The purpose of this increased order was to maintain plant production until March 1943 as stated in SUMIL 9 (no document found) of 24th October. Another follow-up undated telegram stated document SUMIL 9 is only our "general intention" regarding Thompson guns and the no formal request is being given for another requisition. It ended with the following instructions, "We rely on you meanwhile to see that no steps are taken to divert Thompson gun capacity to other purposes before the Spring of 1943." [174]

Another undated telegram to the B.P.C. followed that stated a presumption that 256,000 Thompson guns were "financed under 1st Lend/Lease." The new order of 150,000 Thompson guns from a list of "Outstanding British Requirements" are to be financed from the 2nd Lend/Lease. A question at the end of the telegram asked, "Are we to understand that extra 200,000 shown in that list for later financing is all we can hope for by March 1943?" [175] Unfortunately, "that list" was not included in the documentation but it appears the MoS were preparing to pursue an additional order for 200,000 Thompson guns, if necessary. One reason to pursue additional orders is stated above - to retain the factory production capacity until the Spring of 1943. The B.P.C. replied on December 10th, three days after the Japanese attack on Pearl Harbor, that the first 256,000 were financed under the first Lend-Lease; 150,000 were for financing under the second Lend-Lease. It agreed, "The extra 200,000 is a figure which was based on possible deliveries up to March 1943. However, the position now developing here in relation to Far East makes all previous estimates subject to considerable changes." [176]

The procurement, production and Lend-Lease numbers were finally starting to correspond. The 256,000 guns financed under the first Lend-Lease appropriation, above, are as follows: 8th order – 42,000 of this 50,000 gun order were procured under Lend-Lease. Add these 42,000 guns to the 9th order of 158,000 guns, the amended 9th order of 6,000 Programme B guns, and the 10th order for 50,000 guns to obtain the 256,000 Thompson gun total financed under what is termed as the first Lend-Lease appropriation. The 11th order of 150,000 guns was financed under the second Lend-Lease appropriation.

Personal Weapons

The cry for personal weapons was never ending. There was a realization the security of the United Kingdom would ultimately fall on local defence forces as more and more field formations (units completely equipped with arms and transport for mobile warfare) were shipped to theatres of operation overseas. "The equipping of all ranks in the regular Army with a personal weapon is of great urgency. I appreciate that the production of rifles is a comparatively lengthy and highly skilled process, whereas the production of machine carbines is simple; I am, therefore, prepared to accept as an initial measure the provision of a high proportion of machine carbines for non-field force units." The current objective was "to arm with a personal weapon i.e., rifle, revolver or machine carbine, not only every man in the Army, but every sailor and airman serving on land, and every member of the Home Guard." [177]

---

[172] CYPHER TELEGRAM from B.P.C. WASHINGTON, 18th September 1941
[173] Immediate War Orders, Thompson Sub Machine Guns and Magazines [218/12], signed C.D. Gibb, dated 25 Sep 1941
[174] Two undated telegrams regarding SUPLY 8017 and SUMIL 9, drafted after October 24, 1941
[175] Telegram to B.P.C., Suply 12399, _Thompson Guns_, undated
[176] Cypher Telegram from B.P.C. & B.A.D. Washington, dated 10th December 1941
[177] (WO199/3249) SECRET, Provision of Personal Weapons, Commander-in-Chief, Home Forces, 31 January 1942

from the David Albert collection, USA
An undated news photograph showing a British paratrooper training with the new Thompson gun.

An Inspection Issue

Thompson guns and associated equipment were now pouring out of America to Great Britain and other locations worldwide. However, mass production also had its failings. Schedules, goals, quotas, commitments, pledges and guarantees mean pressure on those pushing the product out the door for needy customers. It was not surprising to find a report regarding some Thompson guns that did not meet expectations - "Sometimes parts are deficient or broken. The hole through which magazine catch faces is burred, making magazine assembly and removal difficult, guns usually dry and sometimes rusty, Butts and hand grips split." This serious situation needed to be resolved quickly. Reinstituting the inspections of Thompson guns when received by the staff of the Chief Inspector, Small Arms, was an option, but not one that anyone wanted to implement. However, military officials in the supply chain were foot soldiers at some point in their careers and knew, "Units likely to be very dissatisfied if they receive dud weapons." What followed was a stern request, "Please tighten inspection on your side." [178]

The report of deficient equipment brought a fast response. It stated that U.S. Ordnance inspected all Thompson machine carbines supplied under Lend-Lease and they have no control over this process. However, the faults they described are being referred to U.S. Ordnance but specific details of the particular guns and shipments are needed. A request was made to "…obtain evidence by expert examination when guns are first unpacked." [179]

A follow-up report was submitted on the inspection issues and stated U.S. Ordnance "was giving special

---

[178] Cypher Telegram to United Kingdom High Commissioner in Canada, dated 3rd January 1942
[179] Cypher Telegram from United Kingdom High Commissioner in Canada, dated 9th January 1942

attention to the points you raise." It believed the rust was the result of the manufacturer using an unauthorized commercial product instead of sperm oil. The problem was resolved with the sperm oil placed back in use. [180]

A 1942 Auto-Ordnance Corporation advertisement boasting how the "indispensable" Thompson submachine gun was standard equipment with "the combat troops of the British Empire."

A New Tommy Gun

Cypher Telegram from the United Kingdom High Commissioner in Ottawa on 10th April 1942:

1. New simplified .45 Thompson Machine carbine developed by Auto Ordnance owning Thompson rights. U.S.A. Ordnance have adopted in place of old model. Change over will be gradual and completed Aug. with no repeat no drop in production. British requirements will receive new model in increasing proportion as change over develops.

2. Advance notice of change not given. Have now seen sample and consider simplification generally excellent. Barrel and mechanism and trigger mechanism components intended interchangeable with old model. Simple blow back action without locking piece. Weight reduced from eleven to nine and a half pounds. Manufacture much simplified. Cost reduced to about fifty

---

[180] Cypher Telegram to United Kingdom High Commissioner in Canada, dated 2nd February 1942

dollars. Sample guns and drawings not yet obtainable from U.S.A. ordnance but an [sic] arranging drawing and sample direct from manufacturer for forwarding you earliest end. [181]

The new M1 Thompson submachine gun had been introduced and adopted by the U.S. military after testing. Production of the Model of 1928 Thompson submachine gun would be terminated and replaced with the M1 model.

One Million Thompson Guns

On September 11th 1942 the War Office "increased their Gun requirements for 45" Thompson to 1 Million and for Stens to 3 millions, including 700,000 for the R.A.F." A handwritten notation on the bottom of the SECRET SUPLY 13231 memorandum sent to British Supply Mission (Washington), "Confirmed." [182]

from the Bill & Carol Troy collection, USA
An ACME Newspicture, New York Bureau, dated August 3, 1941, captioned,
British "Invaders" Rehearse. Troops of the Oxfordshire and Buckinghamshire
Light Infantry, storming up from seacoast rocks, Tommy guns in hand, to capture
an "enemy" mole, during realistic maneuvers somewhere in Northern Ireland.

The M3 Submachine Gun

While the requirement for one million Thompson guns for 1943 was submitted, the U.S. War Department limited the British procurement of Thompson guns to the undelivered A.S.P. (U.S. Army

---

[181] Cypher Telegram from United Kingdom High Commissioner in Ottawa, dated 10th April 1942
[182] Extract from SECRET Suply 13231 memorandum, dated 11th September 1942

Supply Program) provision of the previously requested 208,000 Thompson guns. The British could receive a part of any excess production but this excess was not likely to exceed 40,000 guns. [183] It is unknown how the order for one million more Thompson guns became the basis for the 208,000 figure, above. It is important to note this one million gun order never progressed to the official stage of requiring an IWO.

There was more news. The War Department had "taken unilateral decision to stop Tommy SMG production as U.S. army is changing over to new cheap pattern of SMG made from stampings…" This new weapon could be supplied with .45 or 9mm barrels. The "Tommy gun facility (Auto Ordnance Coy) likely to be switched to manufacture of cal. 30 carbine…" Of course, all of this would take time and Auto Ordnance would cease TSMG production "gradually." The information to date indicated that a "substantial proportion of 208 thousand will be TSMG M1A1." Apparently, the short-lived Hyde-Inland M2 submachine gun was marketed to the British because information now indicated that production of this SMG was "doubtful." The production of the new gun was supposed to be at the TSMG rate of approximately 60,000 guns per month. A "strong case will be necessary to persuade Americans to increase capacity to meet our requirement of one million but in view of change of type you may decide to expand use of Sten to cover short fall on TSMG." [184]

Changes can happen very fast during a war. A new Thompson gun and a new submachine gun – all within a 9 month period. The British Army Staff in Washington acted fast to obtain information. The new weapon did not resemble the TSMG; standard caliber was .45 but 9mm could be supplied on demand. The standard magazine contained 30 rounds and was not interchangeable with TSMG. A Sten magazine for 9mm could be used with an adaptor. The production of "T.S.M.G.1928 A1 and M-1" accessories, spares and both types of magazines "will end within six months." "Twenty round magazine is supplied British only and has been issued ten per gun plus two for first years maintenance…" "Other nations take thirty round magazine. All demands for above must be cabled within ten days." The following sentence was very noteworthy. "No T.S.M.G. M-1 shipped prior 31/6/42." [185]

On February 8, 1943, the War Office began the bidding process "for 300 M3 carbines for trials." [186] The process to obtain the M3 submachine gun must have been prolonged. On May 31, 1944, the British Supply Mission advised they held five M3 submachine guns and were waiting on the 9mm components. Four were to be sent to the MoS and one to the Australian Mission. [187]

The last telegram in the documentation, dated May 12, 1944, told the end of the .45 caliber submachine gun for British forces - "Requirements of .45 S.M.G. in 1945 are now nil on either Stage I or Stage II basis."* A request was made to cancel Stage I submission of 100,000 guns but the "outstanding balance on the 1944 A.S.P. still needed." [188]

---

[183] Cypher Telegram from B.S.M. (British Supply Mission) and B.A.S. (British Army Staff) Washington, dated 1st Jan 1943
[184] Ibid
[185] SECRET CIPHER TELEGRAM from British Army Staff Washington, dated 19 Jan. 43 *Author's Note: This should remove any doubt regarding shipments of the M1 Thompson to the British military. Additional documentation can be found in Chapter Eight – see type of Thompson guns onboard S.S. Mariso when torpedoed by a German U-Boat on March 3, 1943.*
[186] Cypher Telegram to B.A.S. & B.S.M. Washington, dated 8st February 1943
[187] Telegram from B.S.M. Washington to MoS, dated 31.5.44
* *Author's Note: Stage 1 was the financial arrangements for providing aid to Britain up to the defeat of Germany; Stage 2 was the modified financial arrangements for the period between the defeat of Germany and the defeat of Japan, initially envisaged as being several years.*
[188] SECRET telegram from B.A.S. & B.S.M. Washington from MoS & War Office, dated May 12, 1944

The Final Numbers

A review of the ledger book maintained by the MoS for the procurement of "THOMPSON SUB-MACHINE GUNS" contained information reported above and found in the tables included at the end of the story. The double counting of the first order of 750 guns and the omission of the 54,000 guns ordered via contract A-2308 are not explained, nor understood. Notwithstanding these potential errors, the number of Thompson guns procured by the MoS for or on behalf of Great Britain during WW II is 514,000. This number matches perfectly with the Immediate War Orders (IWO) documentation referenced though out this story. Of note at the end of the ledger book are the following entries, "M.P.(c) rec/s to end of '43   526.241" and "Pos[ition] as at 30.4.42   526.241." Apparently, some of "excess production" referenced above did find its way to British forces but there is no indication of any additional orders, IWOs or payments. The ledger book on Thompson guns ends with the following notation in pencil: "1.081.073 [*illegible word*] MPC schedule 27.7.43." The War Office request for one million Thompson guns on September 11, 1942, may be the reason for this entry.

One source of information or documentation that was not located was the actual contracts entered into between the BSB/Ottawa and/or the B.P.C. and the AOC under cash and carry. There is little doubt actual contracts did exist as contract numbers for some of the different orders are found in the documentation. The search for these contracts continues.

from the Illustrated London News, April 25, 1942
Another drawing by British artist Bryan de Grineau, a commercial artist who specialized in illustrations for automobile magazines before the war, showcasing one of the many dangerous jobs the Thompson gun excelled at – clearing houses of enemy soldiers. Areas in bomb-damaged cities were used for realistic training, and in the countryside, whole villages were requisitioned. The American Tommy gun would forever be a part of British history.

Chapter Two: Joint Inspection Board of the United Kingdom and Canada

The Joint Inspection Board of the United Kingdom and Canada was an Anglo-Canadian initiative created in 1939 after the change in the Neutrality laws in the USA that started the cash-and-carry program. Until this happened, no British inspection personnel could visit the manufacturing facilities in the United States. When the law changed the British government acted quickly to contract with US and Canadian firms for war material and establish an inspection operation that would insure the products purchased were manufactured to the contracted for standards. The BSB in Canada worked hand in hand with the British Purchasing Commission to obtain the necessary goods needed during the war by the British military; the Inspection Board was part of this process. The number of employees could be counted on one hand when the Board was created in late 1939. Standards and operating procedures had to be drafted and competent employees needed to be identified and hired. 1940 was a very busy year, so busy that the Inspection Board did not have its first official meeting until November 15, 1940.[189]

The need for the Thompson gun was quickly identified by the British Expeditionary Force in France. From Britain's point of view it was desirable that orders for war supplies should be placed in Canada rather than the USA as there would be no neutrality laws to worry about and payment could be made at a later date when both governments found it convenient. However, the Thompson was a patented article and there was only one source for it. The problem was compounded by the immediate British military need and the original stock of guns was now exhausted. A subcontractor hired by Auto-Ordnance, Savage Arms, was racing to get the Thompson gun back into production. It is not known when the Directorate of Small Arms and Ammunition of the Inspection Board of the United Kingdom and Canada was first able to send inspectors to the Savage plant to inspect this product that was so desperately needed. This documentation has not yet been found. However, it is known that inspectors were being hired, trained and sent out across American and Canada to perform their missions for all products under contract by the British, albeit slowly at first. [190]

The mark used by British inspectors to mark the Thompson receiver that would identify the product as one to be used for the British contract is commonly referred to as the Woolwich stamp. It is a crown with the letter W inside.[191] It has also been noted on other small arms purchased by the BPC in this period. Savage Thompson serial number S-86612 featured later in this story (Chapter Sixteen) showcases a perfect example of this mark. The lowest serial numbered Savage Thompson observed by

---

[189] (CAB 102/37) Joint Inspection Board of the U.K. and Canada, Final Report and Review of U.K. Interests
[190] Ibid
[191] ARMAMENTS INSPECTION DEPARTMENT, LIST OF STAMPS USED IN VARIOUS DIVISIONS, REVISED 1/10/39

author with the Woolwich mark is in the 35,000 serial number range. However, the majority of Thompson guns with this mark appear in the Savage Arms 60,000 to 90,000 serial number range. Much more study is needed in this area to understand fully when the Inspection Board presence at Savage Arms became a full time endeavor and the Thompson guns under British contract were routinely inspected and marked for the British military. What can be stated with almost certainly is this did not happen as a matter of course with the early contracts for the Thompson gun during the early and middle part of 1940.

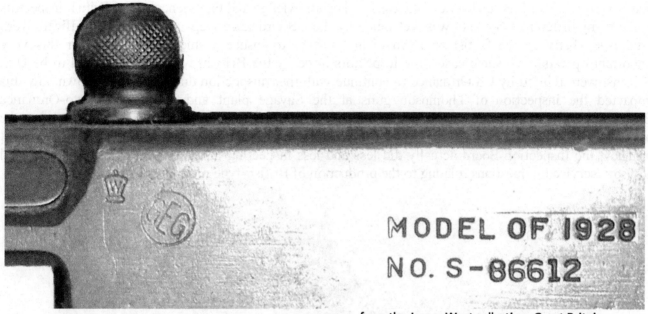

from the James West collection, Great Britain

Savage Thompson submachine gun serial number S-86612. Note the crown mark with the letter W, commonly referred to as the Woolwich mark, beside the GEG mark. GEG or George E. Goll was an Auto-Ordnance inspector assigned to the Savage Arms plant. Close-up picture, below.

When the Lend-Lease Act was passed into law in March 1941, the United States gradually took over the existing British contracts for Thompson guns. This had to be a gradual process as U.S. Secretary of Treasury Henry Morgenthau, Jr. had assured Congress during hearings on the Lend-Lease Bill that Britain had enough dollars to meet existing financial commitments. And the US Ordnance Department took over the inspection duties, much to the delight of the Inspection Board – "It was with no little relief that the resources and extensive powers of control of the U.S. Ordnance were welcomed by the Board when that department understood responsibilities for the inspection of all the contracts taken over by the U.S.A. under Lend-Lease."[192] The knowledge and experience of the British inspectors at the many different US plants was welcomed by the US Ordnance Department. Liaison officers were established between the British and American military to insure a smooth transition for this very important operation. In some cases, the inspectors hired by the British, who also happened to be U.S. citizens, were rehired by US Ordnance to continue with their inspection duties. It is unknown how this impacted the inspection of Thompson guns at the Savage plant and later at the Auto-Ordnance Bridgeport plant. It is believed the use of the Woolwich stamp was discontinued shortly after the passage of the Lend-Lease Act. As the war went on, and the U.S. Ordnance Department assumed primacy, the Inspection Board actually did less and less inspecting in the U.S. but became a technical advisory service on questions relating to the production of British-type munitions there.[193]

INSPECTION BOARD
OF
UNITED KINGDOM AND CANADA

A 1944 letter head from the Joint Inspection Board of the United Kingdom and Canada. The letter head shown at the beginning of the chapter is from 1941.

---

[192] (CAB) 102/37) Joint Inspection Board of the U.K. and Canada, Final Report and Review of U.K. Interests
[193] (AVIA 38/214) Inspection of munitions and equipment: reports

Chapter Three: All that other necessary equipment

The next part of this story is devoted to all the other equipment associated with the procurement of a submachine gun for Britain during World War II. The documentation at the National Archives was so voluminous that each of the below areas, if not redacted, would have interrupted the flow of the story about the actual procurement of the Thompson gun for British forces. Instead of excising information, these sections are told in chronological order with the express purpose of providing as much information as possible to the reader. Expect leaps in time as issues and information with each of these topics arose at different times throughout the procurement process.

Magazines & Drums

New suppliers or competition in the production of box and drum magazines was mentioned in a November 20, 1940 telegram - "In case of competition which has been introduced box magazines now cost 60 cents to 80 cents each and drum magazines average 5 dollars 50 cents each." [194] A MoS ledger sheet titled, "Particulars of Orders Placed For Thompson Sub-Machines etc. in USA," references a contract with The Crosby Co., Buffalo, N.Y., for 2500 drum magazines that was completed in October 1940. Another contract for 100,000 drum magazines with Crosby is also referenced that was completed in February 1941. These two orders specifically reference IWO 218/5, the second order for 2,000 Thompson guns. [195]

The subject of drums became a heated topic in April 1941 when a Cypher Telegram to the British Purchasing Commission (B.P.C.) revealed, "Military authorities here in doubt about suitability of the 50 round drum." "Please arrange to suspend shipment of drums temporarily." [196] This stemmed from a Précis debating the "abolition of drum as an article of equipment." The reasons given were:

a. Mechanically delicate
b. Heavy & unwieldy to carry
c. Difficult for firer to judge when the drum is nearly empty.

The seriousness of this issue was not lost on P.A.S.(P.) G.W. Turner at the MoS. He stated, "…we have definitely ordered over a million and have had over 300,000 delivered, and they are coming forward at a high rate." He further acknowledged, "…this will produce a difficult situation for the B.P.C. and the contractors and we must give more definite instructions without delay." [197] Turner's subordinates at the MoS agreed with the approximate order of one million drums, however, the correct figure regarding shipments and delivery was 783,464 drums. The manufacture of another 180,636 drums was under contract and it was "questionable whether we shall be able to cancel all this quantity." [198] Steps were underway to provide the correct information.

The April 16, 1941, SECRET letter from Sinclair to Brown regarding new Thompson gun orders under Lend-Lease referenced above (p. 36) ended with the following - "…additional Thompson guns should be supplied with the box magazine and not with the Drum." Later in the month an April 23rd telegram to

---

[194] CYPHER TELEGRAM NEW YORK, 20th November 1940
[195] Ministry of Supply, SUPP 4-310 – Contract Record Books
[196] CYPHER TELEGRAM to the B.P.C. in NEW YORK, 10th April 1941
[197] Précis of S.D. 10, (240A) handwritten (undated) and D.G.A.R. Encl. 3 by G.W. Turner, dated April 10, 1941
[198] Internal MoS handwritten documentation No. 256, signed by unknown employee, M.P.C., dated May 13, 1941

the B.P.C., previously cited (p. 36), stayed on message - "…any new orders should exclude the 50 round drum and include 20 round box magazines on present scale." A final decision on the drums was promised soon.

A May 15th telegram, "Decision has now been reached that no fifty round drum magazines additional to those already shipped are required." The telegram went on to state the total quantity of box magazines required was being increased from 1,716,000 to 3,250,000. It was noted the cancellation of the drum magazines would have to be arranged and hoped the additional requisition of 1,534,000 box magazines may make the cancellations easier to negotiate. [199]

The numbers concerning everything Thompson always seemed to be in conflict. B.P.C. officials responded that they "cannot identify your box magazine figures of 1,716,000." B.P.C. contracts were currently in place for 1,452,000 box magazines, 919,000 drums and 108,000 Thompson guns. The B.P.C. had requisitioned under Lend-Lease 206,000 guns, 1,030,000 box magazines and were "endeavoring to cancel" about 500,000 drum orders. The B.P.C. agreed to requisition 1,000,000 additional box magazines "to approximate your total of 3,250,000." [200] On May 28, 1941, the B.P.C. reported that the U.S. was firmly committed for 510,000 drums and "for reasons of good faith and public policy will not cancel." The U.S. was investigating changing the delivery of these drums to themselves or other countries such as China. However, the B.P.C. stated they would not accept any additional deliveries of drums under Lend-Lease unless so instructed. [201] This position on drums was stated again in a June 12th telegram to the B.P.C. Washington.

Everything seemed fine with the British decision not to accept any additional drum magazines. That is, until the B.P.C. asked the War Office if the decision not to procure any additional drums "apply to medium tanks being built in the U.S. which have 24 drums catered for stowage. Going to box magazines means another design difference from U.S. Tanks." [202] A week later it was determined that "no alteration in stowage of tanks is required to house twenty round magazines." In addition, it had been found in a trial that Thompson guns with drums had been "subject to stoppage" so a request was made for sixteen twenty round magazines for each gun. [203] The trials were held at the Small Arms School at Bisley earlier in the year and found that "when drum magazines were carried in vehicles the cartridges were very easily displaced and so produced stoppages." There was a caveat to the report that stated while the Army was discontinuing use of the drums, reports had surfaced that indicated the tank units were still obtaining and using drum magazines. A decision was made to forward this report to the Director of Armoured Fighting Vehicles and "obtain his views." [204]

When the Immediate War Orders (IWO) was issued on August 12, 1941, for the 50,000 gun order, no reference was made to the number of magazines needed. U.S. Ordnance via the B.P.C. requested the quantities needed on September 4, 1941. [205] An answer two days later requested "575,000 box magazines to match the 50,000 guns." [206] This request was held in abeyance a short while because a review of spare parts for all small arms had just commenced and it was believed magazines would be a

[199] Cypher Telegram, Suply 3288, 270/SA/6, dated May 15, 1941
[200] Cypher Telegram from the B.P.C. Washington, dated 24th May 1941
[201] Cypher Telegram from the B.P.C. Washington, dated 28th May 1941
[202] CYPHER TELEGRAM from B.P.C., WASHINGTON, 8th August 1941
[203] CYPHER TELEGRAM from B.P.C., WASHINGTON, 15th August 1941
[204] Minute Sheet No. 313A, dated August 11th 1941
[205] CYPHER TELEGRAM from B.P.C. WASHINGTON, 4th September 1941
[206] Telegram, 320A, dated September 6, 1941

part of this review. [207] The hold did not last long; an amended IWO issued on September 18, 1941, included the requested box magazines. [208]

A letter from E.G. Penman at the Ministry of Supply (MoS) to L. N. Helsby at the Treasury again recounted the situation regarding the cancellation of the drum magazines. There was "no great quantity outstanding on British contracts in the U.S." for drum magazines. However, there was a requisition for 510,000 drum magazines under Lend-Lease that could not be cancelled. That said, the B.P.C. would not take delivery of these drum magazines under Lend-Lease and the US was looking at providing the drums to other Lend-Lease customers and/or accepting the drums for their requirements. [209] Helsby replied, "…in the circumstances we agree that we must accept the position as it is." [210]

The B.P.C. reported on December 7, 1941, that it had 47,000 drum magazines in storage and was awaiting 10,000 more "to complete our order." It had no disposition for this material and requested "shipping instructions." [211] On December 16th the B.P.C. was advised the drum magazine was "no longer part of Thompson sub machine gun scale of equipment" and suggested the B.P.C. offer these drums to U.S. Ordnance. [212]

Another change was also taking place regarding the only Thompson magazine type now on the British scale of equipment – the 20 round box magazine. The U.S. War Department was proposing to change all production of 20 round magazines to 30 round magazines. The B.P.C. reported they had agreed "to accept the 30 round magazine at a scale of (8?) magazines per gun." The B.P.C. added there would be no interruption of deliveries and requested comments. [213] It is easy to imagine how officials at the B.P.C. believed the magazine change from 20 rounds to 30 rounds, especially with the elimination of the 50 round drum, could not have a down side. In Britain, Lt.-Col. Gibson, the A.D.(S.A.) circulated his comments: "It looks as if a Thompson magazine half as long again as the existing one will present difficulties regarding (1) Pouches, Basic and Utility of the '37 Equipment. (2) The Boxes, Magazine, Thompson which have recently been approved and are now in production. These tin boxes pack in their turn into Chests, Thompson, 5 boxes in each chest … it is obvious that 30 rnd magazines in modified tin boxes to suit them will not fit into Thompson Chests. So it looks as if the whole scheme of packing spare magazines for units is completely upset … it seems somebody has accepted this 30 round magazine, and asks for comments after they have done so … sudden modifications like this which react on other equipment are likely to cause considerable inconvenience and should be referred before acceptance, not after." [214] Internal MoS documentation described the change as follows, "It's going to be a great nuisance." [215]

A Cypher Telegram was sent to the B.P.C. and B.A.D., Washington, reaffirming the above complaints regarding the acceptance of the 30 round magazine and made the following request - "Try hard to get decision reversed." Then it politely added, "Suggest in future such matters are referred for comment before acceptance." [216]

---

[207] Internal Ministry of Supply documentation, R. Bryant, MoS, No. 320, dated September 6, 1941
[208] Amended Immediate War Orders, Thompson Sub Machine Guns and Box Magazines (218/11), dated 18 Sep 1941
[209] Letter from Penman to Helsby, dated 20th September 1941
[210] Letter from Helsby to Penman, dated 25th September 1941
[211] Cypher Telegram from B.P.C. & B.A.D. Washington to M of S & W.O., dated 7th Dec 1941
[212] Cypher Telegram to B.P.C. & B.A.D. Washington from W.O. & M of S, dated 16th Dec 1941
[213] Cypher Telegram from B.P.C. & B.A.D. Washington, dated 23rd Dec 1941
[214] Memorandum to S.D. 10 from Assistant Director of Artillery (Small Arms) Gibson, dated January 2, 1942
[215] Internal Ministry of Supply documentation, No 360 from A.D.C.A., dated January 1, 1942
[216] Cypher Telegram to B.P.C. & B.A.D. Washington, dated 6th January 1942

The B.P.C. understood. It responded quickly that the U.S. Ordnance would change to the 30 round magazine as soon as contracts permitted, "But are willing continue 20 round for our requirements." The immediate problem was resolved. However, the B.P.C. went on to state that the "30 round magazine conforms to 20 round except two and three eighths inches longer" and that they had tried the 30 round magazine in the British issued pouch and found it acceptable. The policy of standardization with the U.S. whenever possible "facilitates L.L. action and also adjustment of deliveries between U.S. and ourselves." The telegram ended, "We strongly recommend this policy whenever practicable," but agreed, "no change to 30 round for our requirement will be made without your agreement." [217] The General Staff joined the issue when it sent out a cable confirming they "do not, repeat do not, wish to depart from twenty round magazines." [218] The B.P.C. re-affirmed there was no objection by the U.S. to continue supplying 20 round magazines and agreed to advise immediately if an issue arose. [219]

from the Mike Wank & Ron Brock collections; photography by Julie Wank
**British metal ammunition boxes containing 10 type XX or 20 round box magazines.
One of several reasons the British preferred the 20 magazines. Note the two different
variations of lid markings.**

Approximately 50,000 drum magazines manufactured under contract for the British military after they decided it was not suitable for military service were in storage. The U.S. Ordnance "consider them only fit for scrap." The magazines were occupying valuable storage space; request, "disposal instructions." [220]

---

[217] Cypher Telegram from B.P.C. & B.A.D. Washington, dated 10th January 1942
[218] Draft Cable regarding instructions from General Staff, dated January 22nd 1942
[219] Cypher Telegram from B.P.C. & B.A.D. Washington, dated 18th February 1942
[220] Cypher Telegram from B.P.C. & B.A.D. Washington, dated 1st February 1942

An order was sent to the B .P.C. on February 24, 1942, to scrap the drum magazines because there was "no other useful outlet." [221]

A review of drum orders in the USA indicated 964,100 drum magazines ordered. However, the total was being reduced by 45,000 drums because of releases in previous IWOs. The total number of drums procured by the British military was "closed" as 919,100 drums. [222]

On April 1, 1943, the British learned the manufacture of twenty round magazines was being discontinued. The US War Department agreed to continue supplying 20 round magazines "from stock while available" and would supply 30 round magazines to make up the balance. The new American "SMG M3" used a different type of 30 round magazine with a central feed. "Now necessary we either change our equipment pouches to take new M3 and 30 round TSMG magazines or follow American carrying method which is separate webbing magazine case with shoulder strap." The American case held 5 Thompson or M3 magazines and it was thought that the US War Dept might make it available to the British. [223] A reply on April 29th stated, "Press continuation manufacture 20-rd mags" and stated that the magazine case would not be required. [224]

LEFT: Basic Pouch, part of the 1937 Pattern Web Equipment. Mk.2 version on the left is too short to close the flap on XXX magazines; Mk.3 version on the right closes comfortably. (photograph by James West)

The British Army Staff and Supply Mission responded on June 10th with the following statement, "Situation regarding production sub Machine guns and Magazines in U.S.A. appears not clear to you." The telegram stated that the production of the Thompson would end when the production of the M3 gun reached a "required level." This level was expected in August 1943. The production of the 20 round Thompson magazine had already "ceased" and the production of 30 round magazines was ending soon. The USWD would continue to furnish 20 round magazines for Britain's requirements as long as possible. The telegram further stated that it might be possible to persuade the Americans to "re-open

[221] Cypher Telegram to B.P.C. & B.A.D. Washington, dated 24th February 1942
[222] Immediate War Order, Thompson Sub -Machine Gun 50 rounds Drum Magazines (218/13), dated 23 Feb 1942
[223] Cypher Telegram from the B.S.M. & B.A.S. Washington, dated 1st April 1943
[224] Cypher Telegram to B.S.M. & B.A.S. Washington, dated 29th April 1943

production for limited number of 20 round magazines if we consider vital no 30 round magazines be issued." Also, an additional allocation of 112,626 TSMG's was "being investigated." Confusion regarding the M3 SMG apparently still existed - "This is not a Thompson gun as stated some wires from U.K. recently. We shall receive assignments of this weapon [M3] in cal. .45 when production of T.S.M.G. ceases." The message was quite clear that the M3 took a 30 round magazine which would not fit in the British Basic Pouch; no 20 round magazine for the M3 was being contemplated. If a 20 round M3 magazine was wanted, they should be prepared to provide the USWD "overriding operational reasons" for manufacturing this non-standard magazine. A special M3 "ammunition bag" was being developed; did the British want these? [225]

A reply was sent on June 25th, "Situation quite clear." The reason that the 20 round Thompson magazines had been insisted upon was that the 30 round magazines did not fit the Basic Pouch. This objection was being dropped as the pouch design was being altered anyway to accept the Sten gun magazine. Approval was now given to accept 30 round Thompson and M3 magazines. The M3 magazine carrier was declined, although the British would like to see samples [226]

Review of the MoS Ledger book for the purchase of XX or 20 round box magazines for the Thompson gun revealed approximately 6,144,338 magazines were purchased. While it is very likely some of these magazines were the 30 round variety, the great majority were 20 round magazines. This would equate to approximately 11 or 12 magazines for every Thompson gun purchased. [227]

Spare Parts

The question about spare parts for the new Thompson guns arose almost immediately after the first order of 750 guns. AOC suggested spares of two extractors, "one firing pin cycle recoil spring," one barrel and one spare parts kit per gun. And promised delivery on March 15th if ordered immediately. [228] A decision was reached to order the following "Spares" for every five (5) Thompson guns ordered: [229]

- ➢ Barrels – 1
- ➢ Hammers – 1
- ➢ Recoil Springs – 1
- ➢ Extractors – 5
- ➢ Firing pins – 3
- ➢ Firing pin springs – 3
- ➢ Hammer pins – 3
- ➢ Sear Springs – 3
- ➢ Sear Lever Springs – 3
- ➢ Trigger Springs – 3
- ➢ Short Handle Breech Cleaning Brush – 6

---

[225] Cypher Telegram to the B.S.M. & B.A.S. Washington, dated 10th June 1943
[226] Cypher Telegram to the B.A.S. & B.S.M. Washington, dated 25th June 1943
[227] Ministry of Supply, SUPP 4-310 – Contract Record Books
[228] CYPHER TELEGRAM CANADA, 15February 1940, from Col. J.H.M. Greenly, to Sir Arthur Robinson, MoS.
[229] Initial War Orders, Thompson Sub-Machine Gun Spares (218/3), undated, confirmed in Cypher Telegram from Robinson for Greenly, dated 20February 1940

No money was allocated for spare parts in the first order of the Thompson gun. However, enough savings were found in the monies allocated for the purchase of ammunition that it allowed the purchase of the above referenced spare parts "as a complement to the guns and magazines." [230]

Every order for the Thompson gun also included the same ratio of spare parts. The Initial War Order (IWO) for 55,250 Thompson guns on June 27, 1940, included the following spare parts: [231]

- 11,050 Barrels
- 11,050 Hammers
- 11,050 Recoil Springs
- 55,250 Extractors
- 33,150 Firing Pins
- 33,150 Firing Pin Springs
- 33,150 Hammer Pins
- 33,150 Sear Springs (incorrectly stated as "Gear Springs")*
- 33,150 Sear Lever Springs (incorrectly stated "Gear")*
- 33,150 Trigger Springs
- 66,300 Short Handle Breech Cleaning Brushes

*The mistake or typo of the word "Gear" instead of "Sear" survived into several future generations of lists before the correction was finally made.

On December 1, 1940, the B.P.C. advised that AOC strongly recommended the purchase of extra disconnector springs in addition to the spare parts already on order. The price of the spring was 25 cents each. [232] After much discussion, disconnector springs were added to the list of eleven items purchased as spares in the scale of 100 springs for 100 guns. [233]

The original schedule of spares implemented by the MoS in February 1940 worked well until the passage of the Lend-Lease Act. Talks in Great Britain about a change in the schedule of spare parts for the Thompson gun began around May 1941. The MoS contacted the War Office about a final scale of spare parts to provide the Americans. The MoS suggested to the War Office if their final scale was not complete to let the War Department in America know about any parts that are "particularly required." [234] The main problem with spares is all the parties had different ideas of what spares parts were required. The British, at war since September 1939, were very thrifty in ordering only the spare parts needed; the American scale was much more lavish. Copies of the different spares tables under consideration are included in Chapter Eleven and are listed below by table number:

III.   INITIAL SPARES LIST
IV.   SCHEDULE OF ANCILLARY ITEMS AND SPARES FOR 100 CARBINES
V.   W.S. 14 PROVISION SCHEDULE NO. 9
VI.   REVISED W.S. 14 PROVISION SCHEDULE NO. 9
VII.   U.S.A. ORDNANCE SCALE

[230] Exchange Requirements Committee memorandum, Thompson Sub-Machine Guns, dated 12th March 1940
[231] Initial War Orders, Thompson Sub Machine Guns, Magazines, Ammunition and Spares (218/6), dated May 27, 1940
[232] CYPHER TELEGRAM via WASHINGTON, 1 December 1940
[233] Telegram, 1068 Suply, undated but in late December 1940 time frame
[234] A.R. 2, Ministry of Supply 264A, referencing Cullen, dated May 6, 1941

A MoS internal document to the P.A.S.P. underscored the problem with spares - "Questions of spare parts seem to give rise to great deal of trouble." An overview of the B.P.C. history of ordering spare parts since February 1940 was provided. Simple analysis indicated the use of the American spare schedule (VII) versus the needs of the War Office would result in an "over-order." One example cited showed 31,000 unneeded barrels at about $200,000 in cost. There was a genuine concern that ordering unneeded spare parts on a massive scale could have an impact on production. Also at the back of their minds was the thought that Britain would have to pay for all this unnecessary materiel once the war was over. One suggestion was to supply other customers like China with some of the surplus of spares not needed or wanted by the British military. There was also a concern about changing orders regarding spares already contracted for by the B.P.C. A general plan of action to continue with the original spare schedule and order separately any other spares that might be needed was suggested. [235] The original MoS schedule (III) was actually "more generous" with the parts it ordered while the initial War Office schedule (IV) reduced the number of parts for some items and added a lot of smaller items. For example, the MoS supplied barrels at one to five guns ordered; the War Office requested barrels at one to ten guns ordered. [236]

The July 30, 1941, 50,000 gun order (tenth order) brought an inquiry from the War Office about the quantity of spares ordered with this procurement, especially the barrels. The War Office was informed the spares were purchased "on the earlier MoS scale." [237] (III) The D.D.G.W.P. or Deputy Director General Weapons Production reported that the Assistant Chief of the Imperial General Staff (A.C.I.G.S.) had agreed to a "complete revision of spares for all small arms." It was suggested the War Office form a committee to carry out this work. [238] Discussions about spares continued over the next few months but very little progress was made in resolving the issues.

The schedule of spares came to the forefront of discussion after the 150,000 gun order in September 1941. An October 9th telegram from the B.P.C. citing from a document named Somow 26, "Schedule of spares provided," indicated the accounting for Thompson gun orders had greatly improved, "for 109,340 guns purchased under British Contracts and 206,000 guns under first Lease Lend requisition amounts to 603 dollars per 100 guns." The number of guns specified, 109,340, was correct. It included at least 1,340 Thompson guns from the French contracts taken over by the British when France surrendered.* The USA Ordnance spare schedule (VII) was a lot more expensive - "4211 dollars per 100 guns." A study on the spares schedule was being conducted but in the interim it was recommended by the "Military Mission" (Washington) that the B.P.C. requisition spares for 200,000 Thompsons guns as per the USA Ordnance schedule. Of special interest was the final passage - "Cost of each gun without spares 100 dollars." [239] The reply to the B.P.C. came directly from the War Office and approved the request to requisition spares for 200,000 Thompson guns as per the USA schedule with the notation, "These are urgently required. Future instructions regarding spares for balance of guns will follow." [240] Another Cypher telegram to the B.P.C. was also received from the MoS and the War Office concerning the

---

[235] Internal Ministry of Supply documentation, to P.A.S.(P.), No. 276, by F.C. Penman, dated July 25, 1941

[236] Internal Ministry of Supply documentation, to D.G.M.P, No. 277, dated July 29, 1941

[237] Extract from Minute 142, dated 30.7.41 from P.A.S.(P.) to D.D.G. (W.P.)

[238] Internal Ministry of Supply documentation, regarding M.P.c. (Overseas), No. 308, dated August 19, 1941

Author's Note: 108,000 cash and carry Thompson guns + 1150 Thompson guns directly from the French contract referenced earlier (p. 15) that were shipped to British forces via the S.S. San Marcos + 149 new Thompson guns and 40 second hand Thompson guns provided by AOC free of charge as a penalty for not meeting the delivery schedule for the French contract = 109,339. By simple addition, that is one Thompson gun short, but given the accounting errors associated with the Thompson gun during the war, an error of only one gun is perfection!

[239] CYPHER TELEGRAM B.P.C. WASHINGTON, 9th October 1941

[240] Telegram for the B.P.C. and B.A.D (British Admiralty Delegation); Washington, from War Office, undated.

procurement of armoured vehicles. [241] This brought a direct reply to the War Office from the Director General Weapons Production (D.G.W.P.) on October 30, 1941 - "To avoid confusion it is essential that the only source of communication instructions to the B.P.C. be through this Ministry." The telegram reported the issue of spares for the Thompson gun was being accelerated to obtain a "final revised schedule of spares." It ended with, "Would you confirm your agreement to the above please." [242]

An undated Telegram to the B.P.C. referencing the above October 9th telegram stated, "Our revised schedule Thompson Gun spares is not likely to increase in value even though itemization of schedule may be substantially different." It further added for purposes of discussion, until the spares schedule was finalized, the "value of spares will not exceed 603 dollars for each 100 guns." [243] Discussions at the MoS centered on the unwise purchase of "a good deal of unnecessary material." Examples provided included, "compensators which we don't want at all and 1 barrel per gun" which greatly exceeded their our needs. The MoS believed "the USA ordnance scale will be at least 6 times too big" and requested ordering only the spare parts needed from the B.P.C. [244]

On November 18, 1941, it became obvious not everyone was on board with the directive specifying spares per 100 guns would not exceed 603 dollars. A Cypher Telegram from the B.P.C. and the B.A.D. (British Admiralty Delegation) Washington reviewed a listing of spares sent forth in a shipment of Thompson guns. The spares were as follows:

> - 60 brushes breech cleaning
> - 10 barrels
> - 50 extractors
> - 10 hammers
> - 30 firing pins
> - 30 hammer pins
> - 50 disconnector springs
> - 30 firing pin springs
> - 10 recoil springs
> - 30 sear springs
> - 30 trigger springs
> - 30 disconnector springs (This part already cited above; possible confusion with sear lever spring)
> - 994 box magazines

The above listed spares are the original eleven spare parts approved with each order of Thompson guns plus the later added disconnector spring (See Chapter 11: Table III); box magazines were not considered spare parts but ancillary equipment. The initial reason for the telegram appeared to be some missing cases of guns and possible spares from a shipment - and how to report the problem. A statement at end of the telegram proved very revealing - "WS 14 provision schedule no. 9 not in use here (Table V). Spares have been ordered as above. In future spares will be ordered on U.S. scale (Table VII) which comprises all items shown in provision schedule no. 9 (Table V) but on a much more generous scale. Copy of this scale air-mailed to you. Present situation will be rectified by requisitioning spares on U.S.

---

[241] CYPHER TELEGRAM to the B.P.C. Washington from M. Of S. & W.O., dated 24th Oct 41
[242] Telegram to the W.S. 14 War Office from the D.G.W.P., dated October 30, 1941
[243] Undated telegram regarding SUPLY 11383, drafted after October 9th 1941
[244] Internal Ministry of Supply documentation (344), to D.G.W.P. by F.C. Penman, dated October 22, 1941

scale for 200,000 guns as stated in para. 5 Somow 26, Sept 18th when agreed by you." [245] The bureaucratic war of spares continued!

The MoS and War Office response to the B.P.C. regarding the above telegram did not waver. It explained in detail the reasons for not wanting a lot of unnecessary spare parts. It also admitted the present schedule of spares is small, "consisting of 11 items only," and only agreed to an increase relating to the "variety" of parts. The reasons for staying with a smaller schedule of spares included the considerable experience the British military now had with the Thompson gun, undeniably, much more than the U.S. military. There was also a belief the generous American schedule of supply would reduce the production of complete Thompson guns. It ended with the following, "We consider U.S. proposed scale costing $4211 per 100 guns is wasteful of productive capacity and should be revised downward." Authority was granted to obtain spares on the Revised W.S. 14 schedule of spares (Table VI) for all guns delivered or about to be delivered. [246] R.C. Bryant, MoS, agreed with the above War Office and MoS response in an internal document, dated January 13, 1942, "we are now on a basis of about 8% of cost on spares schedule in relation to main equipments. U.S. appear to be still on basis of about 25% as we once were." [247]

LEFT: A rear sight repaired by British Armorers using what appear to be brass screws on an early Savage cash & carry Thompson in the 23,000 serial number range. (from the Van Alstyne collection)

Of course, this was not the end of the issue. A letter from the MoS to the War Office on January 15, 1942, underscored the need to show the Americans the benefits of the conservative British supply schedule. Information requested included documentation on the original scale, the actual usage, and the new scale of spares proposed. [248] The next action came from the B.P.C. in an "ACTION URGENT" Cypher Telegram. The B.P.C. wanted a copy of the revised British schedule of spares (Table VI). Apparently, it was understood a reduction from the "United States generous schedule" would assist the Ordnance Industrial Service with production problems but "the field service and maintenance and user require convincing." The B.P.C. was going to attempt to bring all the parties together in a discussion so a uniform supply schedule could be agreed to thus preventing a packing and distribution problem. [249] Another letter from the MoS to the War Office stressed the quick need for some good examples to show why the British reduced number of spares was the best approach for all parties. [250]

---

[245] Cypher Telegram from the B.P.C. & B.A.D. Washington, dated 18th Nov. 1941

[246] Two page correspondence /cable to the B.P.C. and B.A.D. from MoS and War Office, SUMIL 23, undated but in early January 1942 time frame

[247] Internal MoS document (365) by R.C. Bryant, dated January 13, 1942

[248] Letter to Major Wright, War Office, from R.C. Bryant, MoS, dated 15th January 1942

[249] Cypher Telegram from the B.P.C. & B.A.D. Washington, dated 20th January 1942

[250] Letter to Major Wright, War Office, from R.C. Bryant, MoS, dated 22nd January 1942

The report (SUMIL 73) containing the new Revised W.S. 14, No. 9A scale (Table VI) and users' consumption percentage in the Middle East for one year for 100 weapons arrived on February 4, 1942.[251] Comparison of the W.S. No. 9 scale (Table V) and the new Revised W.S. 14, No. 9A scale (Table VI) revealed, in general, fewer spares were being requested. Actual wartime usage of the Thompson gun showed that many of the parts needed by unit armourers for repairs were listed as "Recover" or cannibalised from "unrepairable weapons" in the field. . In addition, no spares were needed for the adjustable rear sight as it was being replaced with an "aperture backsight." Examples of reductions include barrels from 10 to 6, bolts from 3 to 1, compensators from 102 to 0, and breech oilers from 10 to 1. One slight increase involved the cocking handle or actuator from 1 to as many as 5. While not stated, it was obvious the Thompson gun was one tough piece of machinery.

A short time later, the matter was discussed with the Field Service Division of the U.S. War Department (U.S.W.D.) using two criteria:

1. Spares for past contracts and requisitions
2. Future requirements

The U.S.W.D. agreed to accept the proposed No. 9A scale (Table VI) as it related to past contracts and requisitions but only as a "special procurement" only type order. The problem with this type of order was it "will mean an extremely long delay, which is obviously unsatisfactory." However, if spares were ordered on the U.S. scale (Table VII), the demand or order could be worked into the current production without "undue delay." As to future requirements, the news was not any better. This would require "the U.S. to amend their existing schedules, which they are not at present prepared to do, since these were considered suitable by the U.S., also Russians and Chinese." One reason the U.S. was not prepared to make a change is because they "somewhat doubt the accuracy of the users' consumption percentage table in SUMIL 73." An inference was made that any change would have to be discussed "between representatives of the general staff." Add to that the U.S.W.D. terse statement, "Auto Ordnance Corporation of America was the sole source of supply of these weapons, and that any questions of retarding production of the weapons by an over-production of spares was U.S. and not U.K. responsibility." This report did not try to hide the fact the attempt to amend the scale of spares was not well received by the U.S.W.D. - "The above will indicate the difficulties that are experienced in coercing the U.S.W.D. to accept new proposals, and again exemplifies that is impossible for direct instructions to be given to the U.S.W.D." The report ended by stating, "action is being taken to arrive at a satisfactory compromise" between the two scales of spares." [252] Obviously, the new entrant in World War II felt it had more experience with the maintenance of the Thompson gun than an island nation at war for over two years - and only a scant 21 miles away from the formidable German war machine.

The compromise or proposed solution involved ordering Thompson parts as per the U.S. Maintenance Schedule (Table VII) - but for not every gun ordered. While the "American schedule…seems wildly extravagant," the plan was to order spares on the scale intended for 200,000 guns but to use the spares to perform required maintenance on 400,000 guns. This would take care of the maintenance requirements for all Thompson guns on order until the end of 1943. [253]

With financial approval obtained, the A.D.W.S. on March 19, 1942, decided to order Thompson spares at 2,000 times the "Total column" on the "U.S. Maintenance Schedule…less the items marked with a

---

[251] Cypher Telegram to the B.P.C. and B.A.D. Washington, SUMIL 73, dated 1st February 1942
[252] Two page report, K.V.T. COPY, Page 3 (378), regarding SUMIL 73, undated but in the February 1942 time frame
[253] Extract from W.O. file 57/SA/1349, Numbers 18 – 21, dated March 16th – 18th 1942

red cross." This order would be in addition to the 11 items already being received as spares and 20 round magazines. [254] This plan did not meet with everyone's approval. R.C. Bryant, MoS, voiced his concerns to the War Office that the solution they were prepared to adopt was not "tactful." The disagreement with the U.S. War Department over the quantity of spares still stood; to accept the spares schedule but not utilize it for all guns ordered, "substitutes disagreement for agreement." [255]

A letter from the War Office to Bryant brought closure to this issue. The A.D.W.S. stated for the record that there "is not the slightest possibility of the U.S.W.D. reconsidering their scales for spares..." He agreed that the large quantities of spares were not needed but noted, "... we must order off the U.S.W.D. scale if we want to get spares..." The cost of spares on 500,000 Thompson guns or 5,000 sets of spares were "22/23,000,000 dollars." The spares in question "are already on the shelf in the U.S.A." Of greater importance, it "is not a material point" to the U.S.W.D. if only 2,000 sets of spares are ordered. Another very important reason to only order spares at a reduced rate: British units were less lavishly equipped with trucks than their U.S. counterparts. "There is enough difficulty in carrying their essential needs. There is certainly no room for luxury scales. This applies equally to [Royal Army Ordnance Corps] Field Park Holdings." The decision to purchase only 2,000 sets of spares was made - "we shall have sufficient spares on hand to last out the life of the entire 500,000 carbines." A final request to Bryant was to inform the War Office when the B.P.C. was given the order.[256] And thus ended the war of spares for the Thompson gun!

The announcement of the "simplified" M1 Thompson on April 10, 1942 brought this response from the War Office, "...hope scale of spares will be comparably reduced. W.O. desire you to use your influence to this end." [257]

The introduction of a "new model" SMG in January 1943 (M3) brought the issue of spares back to the front. A SECRET CIPHER TELEGRAM from the British Army Staff on January 19, 1943, referenced above (p. 50), discussed spares for this new gun and the Thompson gun. Spares for the "new model" were under discussion but should be "small resembling Sten scale." That had to be good news! Regarding the Thompson guns, 527 sets of maintenance spares for the 1928A1 Thompson "covering second year for guns shipped up to June 31, 1942" had been obtained and an effort was underway to obtain 260 more sets.

Ammunition – fuel for the Gangster Guns

The Chief Inspector, Small Arms (C.I.S.A.), requested an increase from 3,000,000 to 3,018,000 rounds of .45 caliber ammunition for inspection of the newly ordered Thompson guns. This request was denied based on an early agreement in the Thompson gun requisition process that no additional ammunition would be ordered from the USA. It was suggested that the inspection requirement be met from the 3,000,000 round procurement "or from home capacity if available earlier." It is likely the home capacity remark refers to the production of .45 caliber ammunition by I.C.I., Ltd, cited earlier in the story (p. 8). Delivery instructions for the new guns and ammunition were as follows:

- Ammunition to C.O.O. (Chief Ordnance Officer), Woolwich Arsenal later changed to Chief Inspector Armaments (C.I.A.), Inspectorate Small Arms Ammunition (I.S.A.A.)

[254] Extract from W.O. file 57/SA/1349, Numbers 22, dated March 19th 1942
[255] Letter to H.J. Wright, The War Office, from R.C. Bryant, MoS, dated 8th April 1942
[256] Letter from A.D.W.S., The War Office, to R.C. Bryant, MoS, dated 11 April 1942
[257] Cypher Telegram to the U.K. High Commissioner Canada, dated 15th April 1942

- Guns, Spares etc. to Small Arms Inspection Department (S.A.I.D.) Enfield Lock, Middlesex later changed to C.I.S.A. [258]

When the first two million rounds of .45 caliber ammunition from the first order arrived, it became apparent to the British military the specified method of packing would not work operationally. The ammunition was packed 2000 rounds per tin lined wooden case in 50 round boxes; the case weighed 100 lbs. Upon arrival, the ammunition was being repacked in "portable tin plate liners" containing 600 rounds. Two liners, weighing only 31 lbs. apiece, were placed in wooden box that weighed 75 lbs. This new packing was designated Box A.S.A. H.29 (Special). This caused a slight delay in issuance but steps were underway to have remaining orders of ammunition from America packed in this manner. [259] However, the manufacture of ammunition was of great importance so this request to change packing requirements was requested to be done without disrupting the production line or shipments. In addition, it was requested the new wooden boxes be made in Canada and provided to the ammunition plants in the USA thus reducing unnecessary expenditure from the dollar reserves. [260]

The BSB in Canada and the United States reported to the MoS on July 11th that the .45 caliber ammunition as specified in Contract A-290 would be manufactured by the Winchester Repeating Arms Company and the Western Cartridge Company. [261] Winchester lots would be even-numbered and head stamped W.R.A.Co. 45 A.C. while Western lots would be odd-numbered and head stamped WESTERN 45 AUTO. Of note, the priming composition for both companies would be non-corrosive. [262]

In August 1940, the British also contacted Remington Arms in an effort to secure more .45 caliber ammunition. The Remington Peters plant offered to deliver 62,500,000 rounds by December 1941 if the British would invest $365,000 in capital assistance for the plant. Deliveries could begin December 1940 with 1,000,000 rounds and increase to 6,000,000 rounds a month by April 1941. The selling price was not firm but believed to be about $22 per thousand rounds. [263]

The new packing criteria for .45 caliber and 9mm ammunition for the Thompson and "Smith W machine guns" had not been implemented by September 6th due to a "lack of specifications." [264]

On September 15th the British learned they would lose the 4,000,000 rounds per month of .45 caliber production at the Western Cartridge Company East Alton plant. The U.S. Government had now entered the market for large amounts of .45 caliber ammunition. If there was a need for a large quantity of .45 caliber ammunition in 1941 by the British, authorization to purchase needed to be provided immediately. The cable referenced the earlier discussions at the Remington Peters plant. However, to make up for the loss of production at the Western plant it would take an additional $600,000 in capital assistance (approximately $1,000,000 total) for the Peters plant to open a second production line. [265]

A lengthy summary of the program to procure small arms ammunition of all types for Great Britain during the war was provided to British officials via a Cypher Telegram dated 8th February 1941. Of interest is the section on pistol ammunition. Contract negotiations were held with Western Cartridge to

---

[258] Typed notation on Minute Sheet, 22, by M.P.c., dated 2Mar1940

[259] .450-inch Colt Cartridges for Thompson Sub-Machine Gun Packing, dated May 28, 1940

[260] Telegram, dated 29 May 1940, from Sir Arthur Robinson, MoS to Col. J.H.M. Greenly

[261] Letter from BSB in Canada and the United States to MoS, dated 11th July 1940

[262] .45 CAL. COLT AMMUNITION FOR THOMPSON SUB-MACHINE GUN, CONTRACT A-290, undated

[263] CYPHER TELEGRAM NEW YORK, from the Acting Consul General, dated 23 August, 1940

[264] CYPHER TELEGRAM NEW YORK, from the Consul General, dated 6th Sept 1940

[265] CYPHER TELEGRAM NEW YORK, from the Consul General, dated 15th Sept 1940

consolidate all their contracts for the production of pistol ammunition with the B.P.C. during 1941. These negotiations resulted in a contract for 272 million rounds of pistol ammunition: 105 million rounds of .45 caliber and 167 million rounds of 9mm. The contract was ready for execution subject to approval by the Treasury. This contract was only with one supplier and did not affect already executed contracts. There was a direct reference to a requirement for an additional 300 million rounds of .45 caliber ammunition. Production figures were provided from 25th December (1940) to 31st January (1941) as follows: Western .45 caliber – 11,530,000, 9mm – 4 million, 12,750,000 (Swedish order), total 28,280,000. Remington .45 caliber – 10 million. [266]

The new capacity or supplier for the requirement of 300 million rounds of .45 caliber ammunition was Federal Cartridge Corporation, Minneapolis, Minnesota. However, this company required $1,845,500 in capital assistance for building and machinery improvements before an order could be placed. The B.P.C. believed Federal could start production in November 1941 if capital assistance was provided and reach full capacity of 20,000,000 rounds per month by April or May 1942. [267] The Deputy Chief of Small Arms Ammunition (D.C.S.A.A.) recommended to the D.G.M.P. that the Treasury fund the capital assistance for Federal Cartridge Company on February 25, 1941, because of the need for additional production capacity. [268]

The term Lend-Lease was used in various ways during the war. An extract from a May 8th Suply Telegram from New York noted that 206,000 Thompson sub-machine guns and 466 million rounds of .45 calibre ammunition have been requisitioned under the "loan lease arrangements." This equaled about 2250 rounds per gun, about the same as the earlier MoS requirement of 2000 rounds per gun. There was an additional request for 2 million rounds for the requested 52,250 .45 pistols. A decision was made to supply these 2 million rounds from the 466 million requirement because the requested .45 caliber ammunition manufactured to "British requirements is suitable for Thompson Sub-machine guns and pistols." [269]

A case of .45 caliber ammunition, 1/626, was removed from a shipment on the *S.S. Kiamita* in Liverpool on approximately April 29, 1941, for further inspection. The case contained 1580 rounds. The agreement for packing of .45 ammunition in the USA was for 1200 rounds in two 600 round containers. A reason for this quantity of packing was requested. All ammunition must have been of high value at this time in the war. A special request was made for the case of ammunition to be returned when the inspection was completed. [270]

Other B.P.C. contracts involving the Thompson gun were coming to fruition in 1941. M3 medium tanks were allocated two Thompson guns and an initial supply of 4,000 rounds of ammunition with a 1,000 rounds monthly maintenance. A decision was made to cut the ammunition requirements in half for the M3 light tanks because it was only issued one Thompson gun. [271] This decision was approved on August 28, 1941. [272]

---

[266] CYPHER TELEGRAM NEW YORK, 8th February 1941
[267] CYPHER TELEGRAM NEW YORK, 15th February 1941
[268] A.C.I.G.S. B.M. No. 2496/3 – S.A.A. 9 m.m., page 7, dated February 25, 1941
[269] Extract from Suply Telegram 3698, dated May 8, 1941
[270] Two page handwritten document Register No. 270/SA/6, A3 (279A), dated May 15th and a TELEPRINT showing return of ammunition to Ordnance Corsham, dated May 22, 1941
[271] Cypher Telegram from the B.P.C. Washington, dated 22nd August 1941
[272] Womos Telegram B.P.C., dated August 28th 1941

Shortages of weapons and ammunition continued throughout the war, especially ammunition. A confidential letter from Major General Lucius Clay of the U.S. War Department to Sir Walter Venning, Director General, British Supply Mission, Washington, cited a Munitions Assignment Board study that stated, "…since the full United Kingdom requirement for Caliber .45 guns cannot be provided by the United States, ammunition requirements for the United Kingdom will, in fact, decline accordingly and further cuts should be possible in the 1943 United States ammunition production program." The purpose of the letter was to convince the British to reduce their ammunition orders. General Clay stated that increased future production "[is] not possible at this time nor in the near future." [273]

The production and procurement of 9mm ammunition fared no better. An April 16, 1943, B.P.C. memorandum to Venning regarding sub-machine gun ammunition revealed British Services were refusing to accept newly manufactured Sten guns "without an adequate ration of ammunition." The B.P.C. claimed the number of Thompson guns on hand with British forces on January 31, 1943, was 271,000; the projected number to be supplied in 1943 via the A.S.P. was 208,000. The memorandum ended by reminding Venning "that while the British are prepared to take Thompson guns with only 1250 rounds apiece, the United States Army itself demands 2,000 to 2,500" as Venning had reminded General Clay in an earlier letter. [274]

Sir Walter Venning's reply to General Clay's request for a reduction in ammunition requirements began by setting forth the British "tabled requirement for Thompson S.M.G.s for 1943" – 1,000,000. He stated 311,000 Thompson guns have been obtained or are in transit as of January 1, 1943. The above quantity of ammunition requested for the "total (rounded) of 1,300,000" guns was 632 million rounds of which 267 million rounds were on hand or in transit. This amounted to approximately 700 rounds per gun which was touted by Venning as "a very low figure." Venning acknowledged the reduction in the number of Thompson guns forecast to be supplied to British forces for 1943 as 208,304 guns. Adding 208,304 to the 311,000 guns on hand would give a (rounded) total of 520,000 Thompson guns. He stated the reduction in guns resulted in Britain already reducing their ammunition requirement to initially 400 million rounds and later to 350 million rounds. Adding the requested 350 million rounds to the 267 million already on hand would give 617 million rounds by the end of 1943. A projected 520,000 Thompson guns on hand or in transit by the end of 1943 would equal 1190 rounds per gun. Venning stated this number was "inadequate for an automatic gun of this type" and "is considerably lower than the U.S. scale for this gun." Venning ended the letter by stating it was not possible to reduce the British requirement of 350 million rounds as provided for in the Army Supply Program (A.S.P.). [275]

General Clay quickly replied to "Sir Walter" that his letter resolved all questions. The requested 350 million rounds of Calibre .45 ammunition for 1943 had now been provided for in the A.S.P. [276]

The United Kingdom's continuing requests for more Thompson guns and ammunition surfaced again on May 19, 1943. A cancellation in the "Russian (U.S.S.R.) requirements for Caliber .45 Submachine Guns" resulted in a projected increase of Thompson guns to Great Britain of 320,930 in 1943 and 90,673 in 1944. If these increases were realized, it would result in an increase of 112,626 Thompson guns in 1943 and 31,818 in 1944. The ammunition supply requirements were not being changed at this time but an increase "may be given further consideration on the occasion of the next regular revision of the Army Supply Program scheduled for publication on or about August 1, 1943." [277]

---

[273] (AVIA 38/349) War Department Memorandum to Sir Walter Venning from General Clay, dated April 12, 1943
[274] (AVIA 38/349) B.P.C. memorandum from Gilbert Walker to Sir Walter Venning, dated April 16th, 1943
[275] (AVIA 38/349) Letter from Sir Walter Venning to Major-General L.D. Clay, dated April 27, 1943
[276] (AVIA 38/349) War Department Memorandum to Sir Walter Venning from General Clay, dated April 29, 1943
[277] (AVIA 38/349) Letter from Brigadier General W.A. Wood, Jr. to Colonel J.A. Davies, dated May 13, 1943

Instruction Handbooks

An Initial War Orders (IWO) memorandum dated February 1, 1940, set forth the first order of 750 Thompson Guns Model 21 AC, 3000 fifty round drum magazines, 5,000 twenty round box magazines along with 1000 handbooks (handwritten notation). These 1000 handbooks were the Edition of 1940 handbook with the New York, N.Y., U.S.A. address. Collectors of Thompson paper items refer to this as the first variation of the Edition of 1940 handbook, one that can be difficult to locate. Recently, some 1940 handbooks surfaced containing a one page insert or supplement, titled, "Information Sheet for the Thompson Submachine Gun, Auto-Ordnance Corp., New York, N.Y. U.S.A." This insert contained instructions as to the appropriate action a user should take during a stoppage, i.e., the Thompson gun failed to feed ammunition or a jam occurred. These instructions, in a slightly different format, were included as a two-page center section in subsequent editions of the 1940 handbooks. The survival rate for this one page instruction sheet insert appears to be very low.

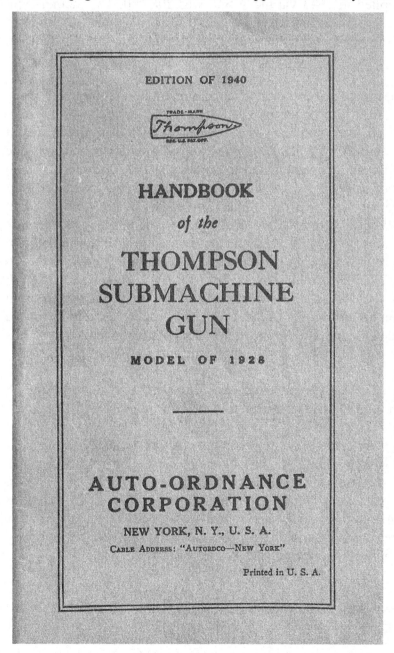

LEFT: The first version of the AOC Edition of 1940 Handbook for the Model of 1928 Thompson gun with New York, N.Y., U.S.A. address on cover. Later editions of this handbook would have a Bridgeport, Connecticut address and may include the Model M1 Thompson gun. These later edition handbooks are much more common. (from the SIG collection, USA)

Shown below is the "Information Sheet for the Thompson Submachine Gun, Auto-Ordnance Corp., New York, N.Y. U.S.A." insert found in some Edition of 1940 Handbooks sent to Great Britain during the early part of the war.

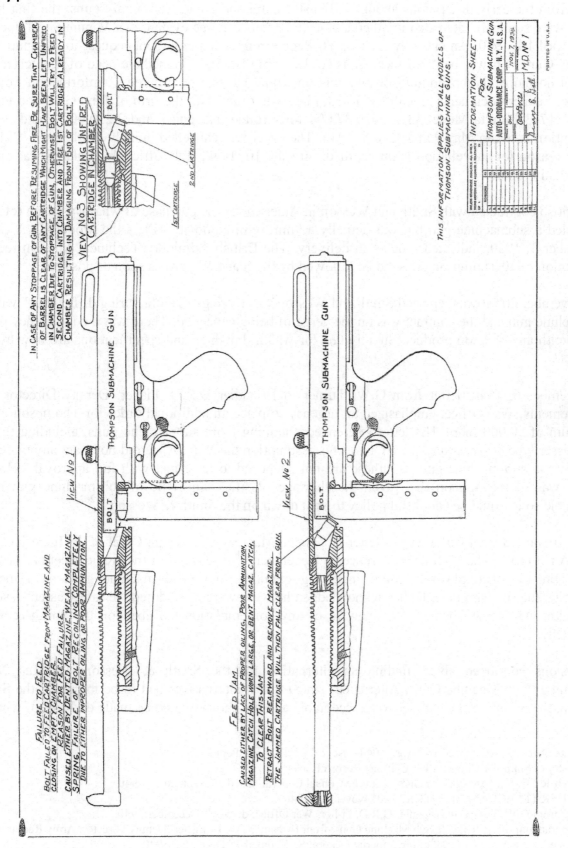

Chapter Four: The Other Gangster Guns

Aside from the early discussions about the Finish Suomi and Hungarian Kiraly guns, the first hint the British were seriously interested in other submachine guns become evident in a Minute Sheet document, dated April 16, 1940. An entry by Lt. Col. H. Peploe referenced an urgent request for the purchase of "Beretta Guns." It was believed these guns could supply Britain's immediate need of "Gangster Guns" and that no more Thompson guns or ammunition would have to be ordered.[278] Information from MoS Contract Ledger documents reveal the British placed an order with the firm of John Gray and Partners, Ltd. for 1763 Beretta Model 38A guns, 37,000 forty round magazines and 2,250,000 rounds of 9mm ammunition between May 9 and June 8, 1940. The order was cancelled on July 12, 1940. [279] While the official reason for cancellation is unrecorded, on June 10, 1940, Italy officially declared war on Great Britain and France.

The British contracted with Smith and Wesson in America for the purchase of what was often referred to or labeled a submachine gun but was actually a 9mm semi-automatic rifle - the Model 40. A cable on September 3, 1940, indicated a delay in delivery. The British Admiralty Technical Mission requested substitution of 50 Thompson guns "to be followed by the S and W guns as soon as possible." [280]

On November 20th it was reported Smith and Wesson was having "manufacturing difficulties" with their submachine gun and the contract was on the verge of being cancelled. There was a contingency plan "to have Smith and Wesson produce Suomi guns for which drawings and specifications are now available here." [281]

A December 6, 1940, letter from G.W. Turner to Brigadier D.R.D. Fisher, Deputy Director, Army Requirements, War Office, emphasized an urgency to place an additional order for Thompson guns - a minimum of 50,000 more. His letter referenced obtaining more submachine guns, including the "new Schmeisser type." Turner also stated it was his assumption the War Office did not want any more Smith and Wesson sub-machine guns as "these are not supposed to have met with full approval." However, Turner was of the opinion that given the shortage of rifles, any type of sub-machine gun may be acceptable so it would be "doubtful policy to shut down on the Smith & Wesson." [282]

Fisher forwarded a copy of Turner's letter to General Macready, Assistant Chief of the Imperial General Staff (A.C.I.G.S.). The letter also referenced a December 4th discussion at the "Rifle Meeting" with Lord Weir, Director of Explosives, MoS, involving obtaining more sub-machine guns as a means of alleviating the rifle shortage. Fisher acknowledged he was aware of a "defective safety catch" issue with the Smith and Wesson but he was unaware of any contemplation "to abandon the Smith & Wesson altogether." [283]

Discussions continued about finding an alternative for the Smith & Wesson. Undated Minutes concerning "Sub Machine Guns. Alternates" stated that if alternatives had to be found for the Smith & Wesson, the Suomi or Schmeisser were acceptable and the choice would be made on basis of which one

[278] Minute Sheet No. 41A, dated 16th April 1940 – No. 3 by Lt. Col. H. Peploe
[279] Ministry of Supply, SUPP 3/314 – Contract Record Books
[280] CYPHER TELEGRAM NEW YORK, from the Consul General, dated 3rd September, 1940
[281] CYPHER TELEGRAM NEW YORK, 20th November 1940
[282] Letter from G.W. Turner, to Brigadier D.R.D. Fisher, War Office, dated 6th December 1940
[283] Memorandum titled, Rifles & Sub Machine Guns, from Brigadier D.R.D. Fisher, Deputy Director, Army Requirements, War Office, to the Assistant Chief of the Imperial General Staff, dated 7th December 1940

could be delivered first. If production estimates were equal, "Schmeisser preferred." Minutes dated December 18, 1940, from the Munitions Production Central revealed this topic was discussed at the Director General of Munitions Production meeting and Colonel Dawes stated, "immediate request would probably be made for Thompson Guns." Apparently the production problems with the Smith & Wesson had "shown improvement and might yet be satisfactory." The question regarding an "alternative can wait until Smith and Wesson trials are over."

Fig. 11—Showing rifle without sling

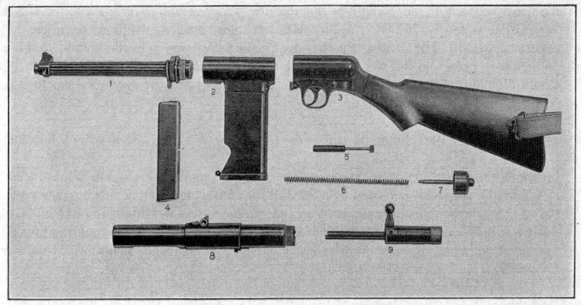

Fig. 3—Showing units dismounted (9 parts)

1. *Barrel.*   2. *Ejector Tube.*   3. *Frame Assembly.*   4. *Magazine.*   5. *Bolt Cover.*
6. *Main Spring.*   7. *Butt Nut.*   8. *Receiver.*   9. *Bolt.*

Pages 6 and 17 from a scarce Smith & Wesson handbook for the S&W 9mm Light Rifle, Model of 1940. (from the Small Arms Review Reference Library, USA)

A SECRET message from Admiralty to the High Commissioner in Canada on February 3, 1941, stated, "Smith and Wesson and Thompson Sub-Machine Weapons were intended for supply to ships otherwise totally unarmed." Future requirements can be met from stocks of Thompson guns and no further Smith and Wesson "equipments" in addition to the 200 will be required at Halifax, Nova Scotia. [284]

British experts in the field of small arms, inspection and quality control were assigned directly to the BPC to evaluate and test weapons and systems offered for sale by American entrepreneurs. The BPC Director, Small Arms and Ammunition, Colonel E.M. Ransford, provided a fantastic insight into these sales calls in the early days of the war:

> We continually received formal and informal offers of imaginative productions programmes and designs and inventions to satisfy any requirements in the smaller caliber weapons – rifles, machine guns, submachine guns, mortars, pistols, grenades, etc, etc. All had to be considered and investigated. Many were accompanied by glossy comprehensive brochures detailing rates of production and performance – some of which reached the War Office and Ministry of Supply in England and were forwarded to us for urgent report. Usually there was little to report beyond explaining that the only resources available consisted of those needed for glossy brochures and salesmanship! The demands for Small Arms and Small Arms Ammunition were (as usual in War) so urgent and stocks and resources so lacking that the British Purchasing Commission was sometimes easy meat for hungry salesman. [285]

Colonel Ransford was very familiar with the Smith & Wesson rifle project and described the following state of affairs:

> In one instance a famous Pistol firm made a direct approach to the War Office in London with a mock-up design of a sub-machine gun and promises of volume production on a rapidly ascending scale. The sample was accepted by the Ministry of Supply for trial purposes only in the usual way but on the strength of this the firm's representative returned to the U.S.A. with a War Office order for 20,000. The promises were not based on available resources in plant or experienced skill. The British Purchasing Commission was prevailed upon to invest some $600,000 in plant and we were faced with a difficult and unprofitable problem in Inspection Control (Quality Assurance). In the event, a small number only of very unsatisfactory guns were produced and the project folded up. [286]

Such was the norm at the BPC during the early days of the war. Another case in point followed:

> In another instance we were asked by the British Purchasing Commission to give special attention to a proposal sponsored by a Senator for converting Service rifles to automatic – a half baked idea which we listened patiently to and explained was worthless, in our New York office. After a friendly interview we were thanked for a frank opinion by our visitor, who said he was interested on behalf of someone who had contemplated financial support – "Would we like to know who it was? – Miss Gloria Swanson!" [287]

The official report to Sir Clive Baillieu of the BPC, dated April 26, 1941, for the above episode was uncovered and provided more details of this proposal. Mr. A.K. Stroud of the "Automatic Alliance

---

[284] SECRET MESSAGE to H.C. Canada , Ottawa, from Admiralty, dated 3.2.41
[285] Ernest Merrill Ransford, *One Man's Tide* (England: Chillingham Publications, 1996), 84
[286] Ibid
[287] Ibid, 84.85

Corporation" made the initial sales pitch. It involved the conversion of a Colt .45 automatic pistol to a machine carbine and the conversion of a .30 caliber Enfield rifle to a machine rifle. The letter referenced a "special request" by Baillieu so the examples were allowed to be submitted for inspection and a "brief" firing trial. However, Ransford politely informed Sir Clive, "there is no doubt that no further action is necessary and we need waste no more time on these proposals." [288]

The March 14, 1941, letter from Turner to Dawes cited earlier (p. 32) stated there were 20,000 Smith & Wesson guns on order for early delivery that are considered "stopgap" weapons. In addition, 20,000 Schmeisser guns should be manufactured from "home production" which will be issued to the Admiralty and Air Ministry. Fifty thousand (50,000) of the new Sten gun should be available by March 1942, out of a total of 100,000 "demanded by the War Office." Turner raised the idea of selling the Sten gun to the Americans but admitted it would be unrealistic since "the STEN gun has not yet been manufactured." He added, "The Thompson machine gun is very well established in America, as you know, and the Americans themselves are not likely to take readily to a new type, particularly as they have an automatic rifle in the Garand." [289]

LEFT: The gangster gun had certainly found its place in World War II. As America inched closer to war, publications worldwide began displaying artist's renditions of the American gangster gun. This early 1941 Dell Publishing Co. magazine cover shows a British paratrooper firing a Thompson gun and asks an important question: Can England Invade Europe? The obvious answer in 1941 - no! However, that time would come soon enough - with the Thompson gun leading the way. (World War Stories, Number 5)

---

[288] (AVIA 38-851) Memorandum to Sir Clive Baillieu, BPC, from E.M. Ransford, dated 26 April 1941
[289] SECRET Letter by Turner to Dawes, dated 14th March 1941

Chapter Five: Diversions

Thompson guns purchased by the British government were not always shipped to the United Kingdom. This was a World War and British forces were engaged in combat operations on many fronts. Shipments of Thompson guns from the USA around the world were referred to as diversions by the B.P.C. The first documented diversion occurred on August 31, 1940. Unfortunately, the documentation is not complete as to the shipping location for these 6 Thompson guns. Shown below are all known diversions, amounts, spares, ammunition and shipping locations, when known:

August 31, 1940: [290]

     6 guns with magazines & 30,000 rounds of ammunition

December 9, 1940: [291]

     guns to below locations with magazines, spares & ammunition

     20 guns to Australia

     145 guns to Burma

     900 guns to Singapore

January 2, 1941: [292]

     40 guns to Hong Kong, 520 drums, 1000 box magazines & 120,000 rounds of ammunition

January 12, 1941: [293]

     guns to below locations with magazines, spares & ammunition

     108 guns to Singapore

     145 guns to Hong Kong

May 9, 1941: [294]

     70 guns to Malta, 560 drums, 994 box magazines & 210,000 rounds of ammunition

     70 guns to Basra, 560 drums, 994 box magazines & 210,000 rounds of ammunition

     50 guns to Mombasa, 400 drums, 497 box magazines & 150,000 rounds of ammunition

     400 guns to Seletar, 3200 drums, 5467 box magazines & 1,200,000 rounds of ammunition

     840 guns to Alexandria, 6720 drums, 10,934 box magazines & 2,520,000 rounds of ammunition

     90 guns to Karachi, 720 drums, 994 box magazines & 270,000 rounds of ammunition

May 26, 1941: [295]

     500 guns to the Netherlands Purchasing Commission, 1000 drums, 5,000 box magazines & 500,000 rounds of ammunition – 1st boat

     500 guns to the Netherlands Purchasing Commission, 1000 drums, 5,000 box magazines &1,500,000 rounds of ammunition – 2nd boat

May 28, 1941: [296]

     500 guns to Middle East, 4000 drums, 6800 box magazines & 2,000,000 rounds of ammunition

     500 guns to Middle East, 4000 drums, 6400 box magazines & 1,000,000 rounds of ammunition

     500 guns to Basra, 4000 drums, 6461 box magazines & 1,500,000 rounds of ammunition

     1000 guns to Australia, 8000 drums,13,200 box magazines & 3,000,000 rounds of ammunition

     1400 guns to Australia, 11,280 drums, 18,000 box magazines & 1,800,000 rounds of ammunition

---

[290] Cypher Telegram from the Consul General in New York, dated 31st August 1940
[291] Cypher Telegram from the Consul General in New York, dated 9th December 1940
[292] SUPLY 45 memorandum (156B), dated January 2, 1941
[293] Copy of A.R.1/1881 memorandum to M. Antrobus, dated January 12, 1941
[294] (AVIA 38/349) SECRET Memorandum to MoS from B.P.C., dated June 13, 1941
[295] Ibid
[296] Ibid

The guns, spares, drums and box magazines set forth in the diversions dated May 9th, 26th and May 28th were ready to ship as per the date specified but the actual shipping date would be governed by the availability of ammunition. A question was raised but not answered, concerning making the shipments without ammunition or without the entire supply of ammunition. [297]

July 23, 1941: [298]

    2200 guns to New Zealand, 28,400 box magazines & spares (later stopped)
    450 to Accra (Gold Coast, now Ghana)
    737 to Freetown (Sierra Leone)
    77 Bathurst (Australia)
    1100 to Lagos (Nigeria)

Many of the Thompson guns diverted as per the July 23rd cable were held up because the B.P.C. contracts were completed. On July 29th the 2200 Thompson guns slated to go to New Zealand were stopped; reason unknown.

from the William Menosky collection, USA

An ACME Newspicture, dated October 27, 1941, captioned, "CRACK INDIAN TROOPS IN IRAN." The description reads, "Part of the British Forces landed in Iran, and now linking up with their Russian Allies, were supplied by the Indian Army. Included were the Gurkhas. Here, a Battalion of these famous infantrymen from Nepal, on active service in the British are of occupation in Iran, receive instruction in the mechanism of the Tommy-Gun. PASSED BY BRITISH CENSORS"

---

[297] Ibid
[298] Cypher Telegram from the B.P.C. in Washington, dated 23rd July 1941

A handwritten summary document dated November 13, 1940, indicates the shipment of one case of Thompson guns, one case of magazines and 15 cases of .45 caliber ammunition to an unknown location. The document further notates a shipment of six 1928A Thompson guns with 6 Cutts Compensators, 6 L drums and 10 XX box magazines on a steam ship from New York to Hong Kong. The Thompson guns are priced at $139.67 each, compensators at $16.16 each, L drums at $10.50 each, and 10 XX magazines at $1.65 each. The total price is $1116.68 less 25% of 249.12 paid on May 29, 1940, for a total due of $837.36. It is noteworthy how the compensators were priced separately from the Thompson gun.

On January 29, 1941, a handwritten memorandum inquired about "any stocks of Thompson Machine Guns and ammunition which are held up for shipping." An urgent request for a diversion of guns for Greece was under consideration. It is unknown if any Thompson guns were sent to Greece, but on January 31, 1941 information from the B.P.C. revealed approximately 9000 guns were available for shipment. [299] A quick reply said to ship as many guns and ammunition as possible over the next few weeks - "Matter extremely urgent." [300]

The B.P.C. always pushed to obtain and ship as many Thompson guns as possible. Accounts were set up at the MoS to charge accounts where Thompson guns were shipped. Even in wartime, costs and accounting of dollars spent were tabulated. The term used was "recovery" for material shipped. [301]

Sometimes diversions of guns interrupted the flow of guns and ammunition to Great Britain. The B.P.C. requested permission to purchase an additional 1665 guns, 4100 drums, 23,000 box magazines and spare parts to have on stock for emergency diversions. [302]

from the David Albert collection, USA
An Australian soldier training with his brand new Thompson sub-machine gun at Chermside in 1941.

[299] Cypher Telegram from Consul General in New York, dated 31st January 1941
[300] Telegram dated February 3, 1941 SUPLY 759)
[301] Handwritten response from New York to SUPLY 507 dated 25th January 1941, telegram SUPLY 1556, dated March 13, 1941, telegram SUPLY 1645, dated March 17, 1941, and Cypher Telegram from B.P.C. in New York dated 16th April 1941
[302] Cypher Telegram from B.P.C. in New York, dated 15th March 1941

Chapter Six: The Home Guard

No story of the Tommy gun in Great Britain would be complete without including the Home Guard. Initially called the *Local Defence Volunteers* or LDV, the Home Guard grew into an organization of approximately 1.5 million volunteers that were too young, too old or otherwise not eligible for military service. The creation of this organization allowed scores of citizens an immediate chance to serve in a useful capacity for the protection of their homeland. Many volunteers were older veterans of past wars; the nickname "Dad's Army" has been attached to it in recent years. The Home Guard was formed in May 1940 when an invasion by Germany was considered likely. After the imminent threat of invasion passed, it was used to free up regular army soldiers by performing mostly guard and local patrol duties.

This chapter is about the Home Guard and the Thompson submachine gun. While the Home Guard was involved in many activities throughout the war, this story primarily involves the Thompson gun. The documentation used comes largely from the Home Guard Southern Command. Records of other commands may exist but have not been located.

The first documentation found involving the Home Guard and the Thompson submachine gun was a War Office memorandum titled: Sub-Machine Guns for Home Guard, dated 19th December, 1940 from General A.F. Brooke, Commander-in-Chief, Home Forces. "I wish to emphasize the desirability of arranging an initial issue of Thompson-Sub-Machine guns to Home Guards and a further issue to Field Formations. As regards the Home Guard, I am advised that there is not much likelihood of the numbers of .300 rifles being increased in the near future, and I consider an issue of one Thompson Gun per section of Home Guard would (a) add to the value of the Home Guard defence; (b) compensate them for the shortage of rifles; (c) enable me to withdraw some of the .303 Ross rifles for Field Formations." [303] General Brooke ended the memorandum requesting an order of 40,000 Thompson guns that would allow for an allotment of 30,000 to Home Guard forces and 10,000 for Field Formations.

Several months later an "Urgent Postal Telegram" dated 5th March 1941, "Subject: - Allocation of Thompson sun [sic]-machine Carbines to Home Guard" was transmitted to the Home Guard commands. It is date stamped 7 Mar 1941 from Southern Command, Central Registry, Salisbury. The telegram stated the Chief Ordnance Officer at Weedon (Central Ordnance Depot) had been authorized to issue without demand 2,000 Thompson sub-machine carbines in the following quantities to the below referenced Home Guard Commands: [304]

Eastern	200	South Eastern	200	Southern	320	Scottish	200
Northern	360	Western	400	London District	320		

Another Urgent Postal Telegram dated 13th March, 1941, set forth the weekly allotment of 500 Thompson guns by the Commanding Officer at Weedon beginning with the week ending March 15th.

COMMANDS:

Eastern	50	Northern	90	London District	80	Western	100
Scottish	50	Southern	80	South Eastern	50		

---

[303] (WO199/3249) SECRET, Sub-Machine Guns for Home Guard, Commander-in-Chief, Home Forces, 19th December 1941
[304] (WO199/1906) Urgent Postal Telegram, dated 5th March, 1941

The additional issue of two carbines for the Home Guard School on Lord Ashcombe's estate at Denbies, near Dorking, Surrey was also authorized. [305]

Southern Command wasted no time in deciding how to divide the allotment of 320 Thompson guns to the various Territorial Army Associations. Weekly allotments for a period of twelve weeks from the Milsea depot (70 guns), the Tidworth depot (135 guns) and the Devonport depot (115 guns) were anticipated soon. Ammunition allotment would be 750 rounds per gun. 500 rounds per gun were to be held in reserve and 200 rounds could "be expended in practice." Two copies of the Small Arms Training or S.A.T. Vol. 1 Pamphlet No. 21, Thompson Sub-Machine Gun would be distributed per weapon. [306]

Imperial War Museum collection
A Home Guard soldier posing with an American Tommy gun, circa December 1940. Note the actuator or cocking knob in the forward position. The soldier is wearing Denims; Battledress was in short supply and not issued to Home Guard units until late 1940 to mid-1941. It is quite likely this is one of the British propaganda photographs where a few guns were shunted all over Great Britain to give the impression thousands of Thompsons were available for use.

A SECRET telegram described how the weekly allotments would be delivered by Ordnance to the Territorial Army Associations (T.A.A.) in a prescribed order. Weekly allotments were serial numbered 1 through 21 commencing on March 15th and involved 80 Thompsons guns per week for a total of 1680 guns. Of note, "the needs of the Post Office and Railway Battalions must also be considered in this distribution." The allotment of ammunition was increased to 1000 rounds per gun with 250 rounds held in Unit Reserve, 250 rounds held in Command Reserve, and 200 rounds to be expended for practice. All

---

[305] Urgent Postal Telegram, dated 13th March, 1941
[306] Telegram, Home Guard – Thompson Sub-machine Gun, dated 15Mar41

reserve ammunition "will first be maintained before any practice firing takes place." [307] Another SECRET telegram told how Thompson guns were being issued to the Home Guard and that the process would take approximately 5 months. Ammunition allotments could only be issued for guns actually in the possession of the Home Guard units. [308]

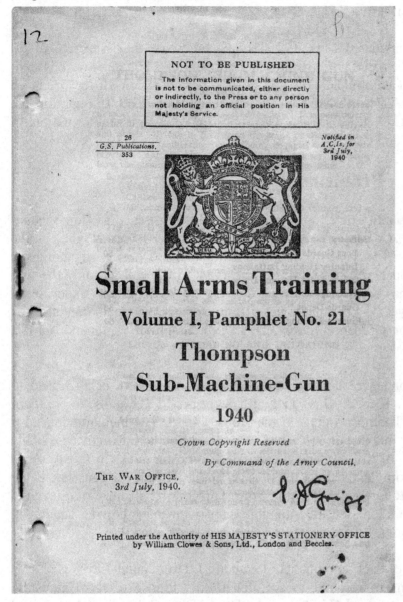

NOT TO BE PUBLISHED

The information given in this document is not to be communicated, either directly or indirectly, to the Press or to any person not holding an official position in His Majesty's Service.

26
G.S. Publications,
353

*Notified in
A.C.Is. for
3rd July,
1940*

Small Arms Training

Volume I, Pamphlet No. 21

Thompson
Sub-Machine-Gun

1940

Crown Copyright Reserved

By Command of the Army Council.

THE WAR OFFICE,
3rd July, 1940.

Printed under the Authority of HIS MAJESTY'S STATIONERY OFFICE
by William Clowes & Sons, Ltd., London and Beccles.

LEFT: A Small Arms Training, Volume 1, Pamphlet No. 21, Thompson Sub-Machine Gun 1940.* (from the David Albert collection)

First the gun, then all the associated equipment soon follows. Approval for the Home Guard to obtain a "Basic Pouch, leather and Slings, rifle" was granted. [309] A request for spares for 155 Thompson guns quickly followed. The following question demonstrated the novelty of the Thompson gun to the Home Guard - "Are Thompson Sub-Machine Guns and Thompson Sub-Machine Carbines one and the same article, please? [310] An affirmative answer was forthcoming. [311]

---

[307] Telegram, Home Guard – Thompson Sub-machine Gun, dated 22Mar41
[308] Telegram, Home Guard – Issue of Ammunition for Thompson Sub-machine Gun, dated 29th Mar41
Author's note: The pictures of Thompson guns in the 1940 pamphlet appear to be of Colt manufacture and are equipped with compensators. The name of the 1942 pamphlet changed to, "The Thompson Machine Carbine." The name of the 1944 and 1944/55pamphlets changed again to, "The Machine Carbine."
[309] Telegram, Home Guard – Equipment, Thompson Sub-machine Gun, dated 15th April, 1941
[310] Telegram, Unit Equipment Spares for Thompson Sub-machine Carbines, dated 3rd May, 1941

On April 25th the allotment of Thompson guns for Home Guard units was increased to 40,000 guns with the following allotment for each command: [312]

Eastern 4,000 Sth-Eastern 4,000 Southern 6,400 London District 6,400
Western 8,000 Scottish 4,000 Northern 7,200

A memorandum from Southern Command dated May 5, 1941, indicated that the issue rate of 80 Thompson guns per week would remain the same until the present allotment of 2,000 guns were issued. The memorandum ended with a hint that communication was not the best between all the ordnance depots and Southern Command - "C.O.O Tidworth has kept this office informed both in regard to the guns received and to whom issued. Will C.O.O. Milsea and Devonport provide similar information, in order that a check may be kept on receipts and issues." [313]

Problems!

On paper it appeared as though a large quantity of Thompson guns were being issued to Home Guard units…on paper. The Territorial Army & Air Force Association of Hampshire & Isle of Wight sent the following memorandum, date stamped 21 APR. 1941, to Southern Command - "Delivery of Thompson Sub Machine Guns to this Association appears to be greatly in arrears up to the present, only the first weekly allotment of 40 – Serial No. 1 – has been received. Can delivery of the allotments under Serial Numbers 4 and 6 – 40 and 80 respectively – be expedited please." Interestingly, this memorandum was not date stamped by the Deputy Director Ordnance Stores (D.D.O.S.), Southern Command, until a month later, 22 May 1941. [314]

What followed were a series of correspondence showing how Thompson guns were being issued to Guard units but not in serial number order. The C.O.O. of Tidworth depot issued a response to Southern Command setting forth the issue of 640 Thompson guns to the Home Guard. The memorandum also stated, "Serial No. IV has not been met by this Depot." [315] The D.D.O.S. of Southern Command quickly replied to Tidworth depot that the C.O.O. of Milsea depot issued 80 Thompson guns "to satisfy serial 4." [316] The explanations did satisfy the complaints from the T.A.A. about Thompson guns not being issued in serial number order. A message to Ordnance Weedon from "Guncotton Salisbury" (believed to be the D.D.O.S. for Southern Command) addressed the situation again with the following statement, "This is causing dissatisfaction amongst Home Guard Units (.) Can you remedy quickly(.)" [317]

Southern Command may have been tiring of these complaints. A Captain J. Drummond-Hay was chosen by Southern Command's Colonel Perkins to respond to a Colonel R.C. Prance of the Hampshire Division of the Home Guard. Captain Drummond-Hay began the letter "Dear Colonel" and explained that Colonel Perkins was "away at an exercise at present." The letter listed 135 Thompson guns that had been issued to Colonel Prance's unit and under what authority. It explained the out of sequence issue of Thompson guns by citing the following information - "…War Office have temporarily suspended issue from Weedon. No reason is given but, as they all come from America the reason can be conjectured." A

---

[311] Telegram, Thompson Sub-machine Guns, dated 16th May, 1941
[312] Urgent Postal Telegram, SECRET, Allocation of Thompson Sub-Machine Carbines to Home Guard, 25th April, 1941
[313] Memorandum, Thompson Submachine Guns for Home Guard, dated 5th May, 1941
[314] Memorandum, Thompson Sub Machine Guns, date stamped 21 APR. 1941 and 22 May 1941
[315] Memorandum, Thompson Sub-Machine Guns – Issue of, dated 3 Jun 41
[316] Memorandum, Thompson Sub-Machine Guns – Issue of, dated 4th June, 19 41
[317] MESSAGE FORM to Ordnance Weedon from Guncotton Salisbury (67A), dated with number "17"

further request to change issuing depots for the Hampshire Division from Weedon to Tidworth was denied.[318]

Another message to "ORD TIDWORTH, ORD MILSEA, ORD COYPOOL" from "GUNCOTTON SALISBURY" revealed Weedon had reported the issuance of all serials but this report does not agree with the reports received from Command Depots. The earlier hint of communication problems appeared to be well founded. A directive was issued to submit a complete list of all Thompson guns received and issued since March 5, 1941, "quoting Weedon control number and authority under which issue and details of issues to formation units and T.A.A. The due date for this information was August 12, 1941. The message ended with the following - "Important that information supplied should be correct (.)" [319] It is unknown why Ordnance depot Coypool was added to the list and Ordnance depot Devonport was not cited.

Documentation indicates that all three depots did respond to this directive. [320] Southern Command compiled the results into a single memorandum. The following number of Thompson guns "have been issued to Command Ordnance Depots for the Home Guard:"

Ordnance, Tidworth   795 guns
Ordnance, Milsea   341 guns
Ordnance, Coypool   352 guns

"It is noted that this totals 1488 Thompson Machine Guns against the complete allotment of 1680." Southern Command directed the remaining 192 guns be consigned to Ordnance, Tidworth for issue. [321] Further review of the available documentation indicated the issue of Thompson guns to other military units, including one to the "H.Q. Southern Command."

After receiving and reviewing all the information regarding the Thompson gun issues to the Home Guard, Southern Command decided there had been an "over-issue of 40 Thompson Machine Guns" to one Territorial Army Association and an "under-issue" to another. A series of memorandums were generated regarding the transfer of these Thompson guns with the result being a cancellation of this determination and an apology, "The error is regretted," from the Major-General i/c Administration, Southern Command. [322]

When everything appeared to be getting back to normal the C.O.O. at Ordnance Weedon issued a SECRET memorandum to Southern Command setting forth the difficulties in maintaining issues of Thompson guns in multiples of 40. Three factors were involved: 1. Increased production, 2. Units mobilizing, and 3. Issue abroad, and to other Services. The production of Thompson guns had increased "considerably recently" allowing the War Office to allocate more Thompson guns to the Home Guard. Increased allotments were based on percentages; these increases were "skewing" the agreed on percentage related to issuance. Factors 2 and 3 were described as a "unknown quantity" not allowing for any definitive weekly requirement, i.e., these events happen quickly and cannot be predicted. Ordnance Weedon agreed "to issue according to your instructions," but added it would be impossible to guarantee.

---

[318] Memorandum SECRET, Home Guard – Issue of Thompson Sub-Machine Guns, dated 25 June, 1941
[319] MESSAGE FORM to ORD Tidworth, Milsea & Coypool from Guncotton Salisbury, dated with number "9"
[320] One Memorandum from Command Ordnance Depot Coypool, dated August 11, 1941, along with three tables indicating the issuance of Thompson Sub Machine Guns.
[321] Memorandum, Thompson Machine Guns, Issues to Home Guard, dated 13th August, 1941
[322] Series of Memorandums from Southern Command and the Hampshire Division of Home Guard, dated August 13, 15 and 19, 1941

It was suggested that small quantities of Thompson guns over the normal allotment be kept and amalgamated with excess deliveries until such time that "convenient quantities are available for issue."[323] No answer to this suggestion has been found.

Suspend the issue of Thompson guns

On September 30, 1941, the War Office suspended the weekly allotment of Thompson guns to the Home Guard pending further instructions. [324] This suspension ended on October 22nd with instructions to complete the issue of serial number 31. In addition, the weekly allotment of Thompson guns to be issued was increased to 120 beginning with serial number 32. [325]

The Exchange

A demonstration of the new Sten machine carbine was held in July 1941 at Shoeburyness* with the Prime Minister in attendance. Claims were made the Sten would be in production shortly with an expected production rate of "thousands a month." General Bernard Paget, Commander-in-Chief, Home Forces, took note of the demonstration and claims of production and requested the issuance of Stens for forces under his command. He claimed the interim scale of one machine carbine per 25 men was too low, but more importantly, had not been satisfied with enough Thompson submachine guns. [326]

A War Office memorandum titled, Sten Guns for Home Guard, date stamped received by the Home Guard on 19 January 1942, revealed Sten guns were initially being issued to only the Home Guard and "special troops" because of a shortage of 9mm ammunition. And not every Home Guard Command would receive the new Sten gun. Thompson guns in possession of the Home Guard were to be withdrawn from most units and concentrated in Home Guard units in Eastern and South-Eastern Commands and the London District because these areas were thought to be first in line should "a heavy scale of attack" occur. This issue rate for the Home Guard had been one Thompson gun per 25 men; this was being doubled for the three above referenced Commands. [327] As Sten guns were received by Home Guard units, Thompson guns would be withdrawn, again, except for the Commands in the Eastern and South-Eastern Commands and the London District. [328]

Of course, what looks easy on paper is often times not so simple in operation. Immediate questions arose about exchanging the Thompson guns issued to the Home Guard for Sten submachine guns. This caused the Ordnance depots to suspend the issue of available Thompson guns pending further instructions. It was recognized that the depots would have "storage difficulties connected with the handling of thousands of these two types of machine guns." A request was made from Ordnance Tidworth to obtain "detailed disposal instructions for the Sten Guns before the 1st Priority of 5,000 are actually received here." An additional request was made to "reconsign" or ship the returned Thompson guns directly to Weedon, "without unpacking and taking them on charge" (creating an inventory). [329]

---

[323] Memorandum SECRET, from C.O.O. Weedon to Southern Command, dated August 20, 1941
[324] Telegram from Ordnance Weedon to Guncotton Salisbury, dated October 1, 1940.
[325] Memorandum SECRET, Home Guard – Issue of Thompson Sub-Machine Guns, dated 22 October, 1941
Author's Note: Proof and Experimental Establishment for artillery near the estuary of the Thames River.
[326] (WO199/3249) 083 15 January, 1942
[327] (WO199/3249) SECRET, Sten Guns for Home Guard, Commander-in-Chief, Home Forces, January 1942
[328] (WO199/3249) 088 14th February 1942
[329] Memorandum SECRET, Machine Guns for the Home Guard, dated February 25, 1942

The only immediate relief that was granted to the depots was to discontinue the "fortnightly return of receipts and issue" of the Thompson gun to the Home Guard. [330] No instructions for the issue of Sten guns had been obtained at the Command level so detail instructions for issuance were not possible. A decision was reached to require the return of Thompson guns to be handled at the depot level. It was noted storage difficulties would arise until the Sten guns were issued. However, Southern Command believed this method would avoid discrepancies "which might involve endless correspondence to adjust, should they [Thompson guns] be returned by R.A.A. direct to Weedon." [331]

During the exchange a call went out to all commands that the wood packing crates fitted to hold 10 Thompson guns were urgently needed by Ordnance Weedon. [332] The Dorset T.A.A. replied on May 28th that all available wood cases were returned with the Thompson guns. [333] The Cornwall T.A.A. replied on June 16th that all Thompson guns and association equipment had been returned to Ordnance depots. [334] The Devon T.A.A. replied on July 20th that 718 Carbines sub-machine .45 had been returned to the C.O.O. of Coypool depot.

Official approval of the "Sten Machine Carbine 9mm. for all forces at Home, in place of the Thompson" was set forth in a 21st December 1942 War Office memorandum. The Mark III Sten was to be the only machine carbine issued to field forces (this aspiration seems not to have been quite achieved in practice). The ammunition shortage had been resolved but problems still existed. Certain lots of British manufactured 9mm ammunition was causing problems when fired "single shot." (The 9mm Mk.2z cartridge - approved in Sept. 1943 – had a velocity of 1300 fps at 60ft from the muzzle, increased from 1200 fps for the Mk.1z. [335]) Field Force units were being issued only American manufactured ammunition. Of note was the caveat that "the issue of Stens to regular forces should take precedent over further issue to the Home Guard." [336]

Southern Command was quite efficient in making the exchange. The swap was completed on or about October 7, 1942, and the order given to "Expedite return of Thompson carbines to Weedon and report completion to this office." [337]

It appeared some in the Home Guard may have liked the Thompson gun more than the Stens and were a little slow in returning the gangster gun. A 18th March 1943 "URGENT MEMORANDUM" with the subject line - "Issue of Stens & withdrawal of Thompsons from Home Guard" told how 7 Thompson guns were still being held in Southern Command. The request, "Will you please have them withdrawn and returned to Weedon without delay" was made at the end of the memorandum. [338] A series of messages identified the location of the 7 guns and "fifty magazines" and told of their departure to Weedon. [339]

---

[330] Memorandum SECRET, Thompson Sub M.G.s (201A), dated 27th February, 1942
[331] Memorandum SECRET, Thompson Sub M.G.s (203A), dated 27th February, 1942
[332] Teletype to all Home Guard Commands from C.O.O. Weedon, dated May 21, 1942
[333] Memorandum, Packing Cases, dated 28 May 1942
[334] Memorandum, Withdrawal of T.S.M.G.s, dated 11th June, 1942
[335] P. Labbett, History and Development of the 9mm x19 Parabellum Ammunition in Britain, privately published, 1996
[336] (WO199/3249) SECRET, War Office memorandum by Director of Weapons & Vehicles, 21st December, 1942
[337] Telegram date stamped 9 OCT 1942, by D.D.O.S., Southern Command
[338] URGENT MEMORANDUM, from Warstore London to Southern Command, dated 18th March 1943
[339] Series of Memorandums from units in Southern Command, dated 24th March and 19 April 1943

The final numbers...

A SECRET War Office memorandum dated 10th July 1942 summarized the use of the Thompson gun with the Home Guard - "Total number of T.S.M.Gs held in Home Guard is 37,290." The authorization of 40,000 Thompson guns was almost accomplished before the decision to withdraw the Thompson gun in favor of the Sten was implemented. While no explanations were cited for the exchange, it was obvious the number of authorized Sten guns (242,412) versus the number of authorized Thompson guns (40,000) was the reason. Apparently, Sten guns were becoming plentiful and were manufactured locally. There would never be enough available Thompson guns from America to fully equip the Home Guard. Another deciding factor for the exchange may have been the availability of 9mm ammunition. The Home Guard had amassed an inventory of 34 million rounds of 9mm ammunition and was authorized 242,412 Sten guns. The Sten was issued on a scale of one per 6 men with an allotment of 130 r.p.g. or rounds per gun. Whatever the reasons, the exchange of Thompsons for Stens was well underway. [340]

Review of monthly reports from the different Home Guard Commands show the total number of Thompson guns in possession did exceed 40,000 in April 1942: 43,017. Shown below is a compilation of various monthly reports showing the reported strength of soldiers and number of Thompson guns in possession of the Home Guard from April 1, 1941 through November 30, 1942. Review of these reports reveal a great disparity of issuance for the Thompson gun in many of the Home Guard Commands. For some commands, the Thompson gun was only in inventory a short while; other commands measured the use of the Thompson gun in years.

The Bernards Publishers, LTD - *Manual of Modern Automatic Guns* – Specially Prepared for Home Guard & Service Use, circa 1942.

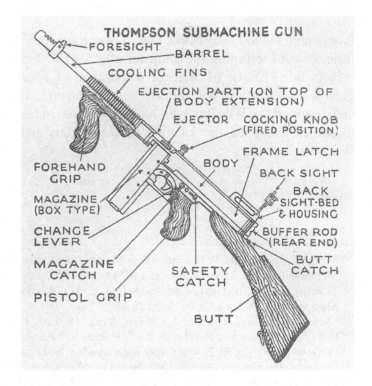

---

[340] SECRET War Office memorandum from Director of Weapons & Vehicles, dated 10th July 1942

Compilation of monthly reports showing strength of Home Guard and number of Thompson guns in possession as reported by Territorial Army Associations between 1st April 1941 and 31st Dec 1941.

Command	1-Apr-41 Personnel Strength	1-Apr-41 TSMGs	1-May-41 Personnel Strength	1-May-41 TSMGs	1-Jun-41 Personnel Strength	1-Jun-41 TSMGs	1-Jul-41 Personnel Strength	1-Jul-41 TSMGs	1-Aug-41 Personnel Strength	1-Aug-41 TSMGs
SOUTHERN	220046	160	218539	720	not reported	900	217558	1120	216131	1364
NORTHERN	307890	535	308157	892	not reported	1247	309064	1414	306545	1945
SCOTTISH	168598	0	166412	315	not reported	571	164712	752	163645	876
WESTERN	516200	93	515640	655	not reported	1124	512393	1209	508306	1953
EASTERN	99976	0	100204	260	not reported	620	100986	807	100880	956
S. EASTERN*	81359	20	81293	890	not reported	1148	93808	1285	92473	1498
LONDON DIST.	203827	386	203855	720	not reported	800	204612	1120	204973	1574
GRAND TOTAL	1610977	1114	1606950	4452	not reported	6410	1603133	7707	1592953	10166

Command	1-Sep-41 Personnel Strength	1-Sep-41 TSMGs	30-Sep-41 Personnel Strength	30-Sep-41 TSMGs	31-Oct-41 Personnel Strength	31-Oct-41 TSMGs	30-Nov-41 Personnel Strength	30-Nov-41 TSMGs	31-Dec-41 Personnel Strength	31-Dec-41 TSMGs
SOUTHERN	214839	1979	197861	2695	196995	2695	195047	3014	192966	4095
NORTHERN	304906	2832	285524	3127	283462	3145	230000	3809	276089	5083
SCOTTISH	161537	1009	160026	1390	159813	1718	159099	1859	157994	2205
WESTERN	503381	2353	503356	2759	495826	3010	492048	3482	484825	4673
EASTERN	100556	1156	134369	2014	134871	2192	134251	2524	133433	2731
S. EASTERN*	90789	1669	89314	3218	88428	2264	87283	2512	86714	2939
LONDON DIST.	202929	2086	202455	2790	200691	2926	198389	3460	195747	4863
GRAND TOTAL	1578937	13084	1572905	16993	1560106	17970	1546117	20660	1527768	26591

* includes ALDERSHOT Command

Compilation of monthly reports showing strength of Home Guard and number of Thompson guns in possession as reported by Territorial Army Associations between 31st Jan 1942 and 30th Nov 1942.

Command	31-Jan-42 Personnel Strength	31-Jan-42 TSMGs	28-Feb-42 Personnel Strength	28-Feb-42 TSMGs	31-Mar-42 Personnel Strength	31-Mar-42 TSMGs	30-Apr-42 Personnel Strength	30-Apr-42 TSMGs	31-May-42 Personnel Strength	31-May-42 TSMGs	30-Jun-42 Personnel Strength	30-Jun-42 TSMGs
SOUTHERN	188340	4939	176413	5376	178365	5037	182352	3568	184504	1038	188546	0
NORTHERN	269854	5507	250852	5926	254567	6455	262615	6455	265820	1496	265700	5
SCOTTISH	156291	2434	142218	2875	144417	3013	149803	1878	152351	592	153931	66
WESTERN	476759	5261	437811	5876	431950	5925	443949	3894	461467	583	468707	138
EASTERN	132173	3267	126132	3795	129683	4616	135230	5992	149992	9835	168895	10069
S. EASTERN*	85338	3338	81189	3784	81994	4036	85126	6746	90463	7080	100030	7119
LONDON DIST.	193559	5356	180964	5889	185640	6886	192806	14484	199966	14574	199037	14431
GRAND TOTAL	1502371	30102	1395579	33531	1406616	35968	1451881	43017	1504563	35198	1544846	31828

Command	31-Jul-42 Personnel Strength	31-Jul-42 TSMGs	31-Aug-42 Personnel Strength	31-Aug-42 TSMGs	30-Sep-42 Personnel Strength	30-Sep-42 TSMGs	31-Oct-42 Personnel Strength	31-Oct-42 TSMGs	30-Nov-42 Personnel Strength	30-Nov-42 TSMGs
SOUTHERN	196262	0	202453	0	206039	0	212101	0	215590	0
NORTHERN	269976	1	278597	1	284191	1	285453	1	283970	1
SCOTTISH	158308	66	161098	26	161113	7	162889	7	163465	7
WESTERN	482859	10	496705	2	499019	5	497467	5	491729	0
EASTERN	182002	10253	188939	10777	192714	7493	195962	4941	198092	2542
S. EASTERN*	107780	7091	112456	7090	115159	6238	120428	2985	122877	2886
LONDON DIST.	202351	14368	206155	12521	205554	10657	205915	9553	205743	7459
GRAND TOTAL	1599539	31789	1646401	29757	1663789	24401	1680205	17486	1681466	12805

Chapter Seven: Winston Churchill and the Thompson

Long after the war ended, it was disclosed Prime Minister Winston Churchill and President Franklin D. Roosevelt corresponded with each other on a very frequent basis. Over 1700 letters and messages between these great leaders were sent and received during the war. One message dated March 29, 1941, from Prime Minister Churchill referred to the Thompson gun. "I have today made allotments for substantial quantities of food and for immediate purchase [of] fifty-four hundred airplanes, four hundred thousand Thompson submachine guns, thirty-four hundred Universal carriers, and substantial quantities of other miscellaneous military equipment. I have also authorized fifty-five hundred Oerlikon guns and ammunition for them, sixty patrol bombing planes, and one hundred eighty Navy fighting planes. These actions will be followed in the near future as soon as I have had the opportunity to confer with your representatives and their opposites in our Government. You can be sure these matters will be prosecuted vigorously here." [341] This correspondence happened shortly after the passage of the Lend-Lease Act. Obviously, Prime Minister Churchill understood this piece of legislation would provide the means to obtain all the necessary war material to win the war. While the list of needed American equipment was long, the second item on the list as set forth in a personal letter from Churchill to the President of the United States of America was 400,000 Thompson submachine guns. This may well explain why the ranking British military officers involved in the procurement process spoke often of an unofficial total of 500,000 Thompson guns. After the direct purchase of 108,000 guns under cash and carry, 400,000 more Thompson guns would more than equal the half million Prime Minister Churchill thought necessary to equip British forces. The final procurement numbers reveal his directive became a reality.

 One of the most widely circulated photographs of World War II is Prime Minister Churchill holding a Thompson gun. A quick visit to the gift shop at the Imperial War Museum (IWM) in London will find this image available on posters, t-shirts, coffee cups and candy bars. An Internet search with the search words "Winston Churchill Thompson gun" will bring up numerous websites with some variation of this picture. Information from the IWM lists the photographer as War Office official photographer Captain Horton. The IWM inventory number for what appears to be the original picture is H 2646, one of the Prime Minister holding the Thompson gun with his left hand on the drum magazine along with accompanying soldiers and officials. The official description is as follows: *The Prime Minister Winston Churchill inspects a 'Tommy gun' while visiting coastal defence positions near Hartlepool on 31 July 1940.* IWM photograph number H 2646A is a crop of this famous picture that shows only Churchill and the Thompson gun. It appears Captain Horton took several different pictures of Churchill with and around British Troops holding this American gangster gun that summer day in 1940. It is unknown if these other pictures are included in the IWM collection. What can be determined just from the date of the picture is the Thompson gun was of early Savage manufacture, probably from the first or second order of guns.

This famous photograph by Captain Horton was published in a 32 page booklet used to introduce the Canadians to Winston Churchill. The following excerpt is from author John Collingwood Reade:

> The British have found a man to lead them – a man who knows their hearts, a man in whose mouth is the rich English tongue, and in whose veins flows the blood of great adventurers. Centred on this man are the hopes of free-born men the world over. In him they place their faith, not alone because of this personal strength and genius, but because it falls to his lot to waken Britain's greatness from its long sleep and summon her genius from the distant past. This man is

---

[341] Francis L. Loewenheim, Harold D. Jones, and Manfred Jonas, eds., *Roosevelt and Churchill: Their Secret Wartime Correspondence* (New York: Saturday Review Press; E.P. Dutton, 1975), 136

England as England must be; and in this moment the people will follow him as they would no other, giving him their best. This embodiment of Britain's genius, this dragon-slaying knight of the cross of St. George, is Winston Spencer Churchill. [342]

TRYING OUT A TOMMY GUN
One of the most famous photographs of World War II.
Prime Minister (and dragon slayer) Winston Churchill
"trying out" a Thompson submachine gun. [343]

Captain Horton or the British censors most likely never envisioned the German use of this picture to highlight Churchill as a gangster - but that is exactly what Axis forces did. A leaflet titled, "FOR INCITEMENT TO MURDER," showing the Prime Minister in his now famous pose with an American gangster gun was being air dropped over England in an attempt to demoralize the British populace and anyone that would listen. Also shown on the following page is the reverse side of an original leaflet. [344]

---

[342] John Collingwood Reade, *Man of Valor Winston Spencer Churchill* (Canada: Rous & Mann Limited, 1941), 5
[343] Reade, 16
[344] *The War Weekly*, No. 54, 1 November, 1940

WANTED

FOR INCITEMENT TO
MURDER

This is on one side of a leaflet which German planes have been dropping over parts of East Anglia and elsewhere in England. On the other side are these words: "The gangster who you see in his element in the picture incites you by his example to participate in a form of warfare in which women, children and ordinary civilians shall take leading parts. This absolutely criminal form of warfare, which is forbidden by The Hague Convention, will be punished according to military law. Save at least your families from the horror of war!" It is ironical that the Germans, who have broken every law of warfare, should invoke the Hague Convention now.

This gangster, who you see in his element in the picture, incites you by his example to participate in a form of warfare in which women, children and ordinary civilians shall take leading parts.

This absolutely criminal form of warfare which is forbidden by the

HAGUE CONVENTION

will be punished

according to military law

Save at least your families from the horrors of war!

The German war machine did not stop with leaflets. Pictures of the Churchill with or around troops armed with this gangster gun were featured in German newspapers. Shown on the following page is the September 5, 1940, front page of the *Munich Illustrated Press,* a German newspaper. The caption reads, "He Collects New Material for New Speeches. A new machine gun is being explained to Mr. Winston Churchill. His questions seemed to have unnerved the officer standing next to him." The expression on the British officer's face certainly confirms the description! This paper appears to have had a wide circulation as prices are listed on the cover for the following countries: Italy, Switzerland, Yugoslavia, Holland, Estonia, Belgium and Latvia.

from the Lawrence Augustus collection, USA

Translation by Carol Troy and the Fairfax Parks and Recreation's German Speakers Group

Another interesting story involving the Thompson gun is told by William Shawcross in Queen Elizabeth The Queen Mother: The Official Biography (2009):

"Joseph P. Kennedy, the US Ambassador in London, noted in his diary [345] a story told him by Brendan Bracken, now a minister in the government. On one of Churchill's weekly visits to the King at Buckingham Palace he found him in the garden shooting at a target with a rifle. The King told his Prime Minister that 'if the Germans were coming, he was at least going to get his German, and Churchill said if he felt that way about it, he would get him a Tommy Gun so he could kill a lot of Germans and he is getting him one' "

The American Tommy gun had certainly found acceptance in Great Britain.

from the American Thompson Reference Collection, USA

King George VI apparently did get his Thompson gun as he is featured in a news photograph, circa 1941, titled: "King Tries a Tommy Gun." The caption tells about how the King "goes into action" with a Tommy Gun on a range at the Southern Command station. The King did not do very well shooting from the shoulder (as shown) but later hit the bulls-eye when firing from the hip.

---

[345] Joseph P. Kennedy, *Hostage To Fortune: The Letters of Joseph P. Kennedy* (USA: Viking Adult, 2001) 457

Chapter Eight: The U-Boats!

The number of Thompson guns purchased by Great Britain under cash and carry is fairly certain: 108,000. The remaining balance was obtained as a result of the French contracts and under Lend-Lease. The total number from all sources is far from certain but solid evidence exists the total is at least 514,000 – and most likely as high as 526,241 guns. The question that always arises is how many Thompson guns actually survived shipment to Great Britain or other locations. Pundits on both sides of the Atlantic have offered various figures over the years as to how many Thompson guns are at the bottom of the ocean. However, none has produced any supporting documentation. The consensus of losses from noted authors are general claims of "a sizeable percentage" or "quite a few." One author cites the delivery of only 100,000 of the 514,000 guns procured. Never disclosed is how anyone arrived at any answer – until now. Presented below is some solid evidence of losses that will allow a reader to utilize facts when answering this long-standing question.

The "Pre Lease Lend Requirements" table cited earlier in the story and presented at the end of this chapter not only shows orders of Thompson guns but losses in transit for the 108,000 Thompsons guns ordered by the MoS under cash and carry. It is not surprising the MoS was very interested in the number of Thompson guns ordered and received under cash and carry. They understood there was no guarantee when a shipment of Thompson guns departed New York harbor that the guns would arrive at the intended destination. Simple economics dictates knowledge of losses is important to accurately predict future requirements. The more losses, the more orders will be needed in the future. Given this table was completed in real time when the outcome of the war was far from certain, it must be viewed at a minimum as the best effort of MoS employees. Of the 108,000 Thompson guns purchased directly from AOC, 4,950 were known to be lost in transit. That is a loss rate of approximately 4.6%.

It is also important to know the time frame involved with the production and delivery of the first 108,000 guns. As reported earlier (p. 36), Savage had only manufactured 84,780 guns by the end of March 1941. We also learned on July 23, 1941 that all B.P.C. Thompson gun contracts had been completed. Unfortunately, the exact date when the cash and carry contracts were completed is not known. But it has to be sometime between April 1, 1941 and July 23, 1941. All Thompson guns obtained by British forces after that were under Lend-Lease.

Research at the National Archives revealed several files on the shipping losses suffered by the British government because of the vast German U-Boat campaign during the war. The files were generally divided into lists of shipping losses of "Manufactured Stores" and "Raw Material" as a result of enemy action. Detailed cargo manifests of total losses were sent to the B.P.C. to enable them to balance their books and reorder lost equipment, if necessary. The lists were usually divided into two groups, "Ships Proceeding to other than U.K. Ports" and "Ships Proceeding to U.K. Ports." Also inside the file was a copy of Admiralty Book of Reference B.R.1337, *"British & Foreign Merchant Vessels Lost Or Damaged By Enemy Action During The Second World War."* This bound book, intended for official use only, was issued by the Admiralty Trade Division in November 1945, as a definitive statement of losses with name, flag, propulsion type, tonnage, date, cause, position where known, etc. Any conflict of information has been resolved by using B.R. 1337. The first loss of 2000 Thompson guns is recorded on October 17, 1941. Based on when the B.P.C. cash & carry contracts ended and Lend-Lease began, it is safe to assume these would have been Lend-Lease Thompsons. Losses of Thompson guns and equipment associated with the Thompson gun continue until August 28, 1943. [346]

---

[346] (AVIA 22/3321) Lost Cargo; Weekly Returns and B.R. 1337 (Restricted) 1945

A table detailing the losses is included at the end of this chapter. Review of the losses indicates 22,358 Thompson guns were lost to enemy action from October 17, 1941, through March 20, 1943. Using 514,000 as a conservative number of Thompson guns procured by the MoS and subtracting the first 108,000 guns obtained under cash and carry leaves a balance of 406,000. Of the 406,000 Thompson guns obtained from America under Lend-Lease, 22,358 were known to be lost in transit. This is a loss rate of approximately 5.5%.

It must be noted that while the production of the Thompson gun officially ended in February 1944, only 4,091 guns were manufactured in 1944. December 1943 was the last month of what appeared to be a full production schedule. [347] This fits perfectly within the time frame of known shipping loss documentation for the Thompson gun found at the National Archives, above. A simple review of Allied shipping losses by U-boat activity shows the rate of loss slowed considerably toward the end of 1943. In addition, except for the losses in transit documented on the table of Pre Lease Lend Requirements, there is no mention in any of the files or documentation expressing even an acknowledgement regarding losses. Certainly, if losses of the Thompson gun by shipping would have been paramount, it would have been noteworthy and at the very least caused increased orders. The main reason cited over and over again for the increased orders of Thompson guns was the shortage of rifles.

It must be emphatically stated that it is unknown if all the shipping losses are accounted for in this actual documentation. However, what can be proved now are the shipping losses for the 108,000 cash & carry Thompsons guns was 4.6%. And the shipping losses for at least 406,000 Lend-Lease Thompson guns was 5.5%. This low rate may explain why no documentation was found at the MoS lamenting excessive shipping losses of Thompson guns during transit.

A list of abbreviations used in the tables on the following pages: **Ships Lost Carrying Thompson Submachine Guns**

G.T.   gross tonnage
S.M.   submarine
A.C.   aircraft
S.   steamship
T.   torpedo
M.   motor vessel
*   presumed

The line items in the chart on page 96 correspond to the same line item on the chart on page 97. The ship's name is provided in the first column of both charts for ease of reference. This same format is followed for the charts on pages 98 and 99.

---

[347] Iannamico, 166

Ships Lost Carrying Thompson Submachine Guns

Ship	G.T.	Type of propulsion	Flag	Port of Departure	Destination	No. of guns	Accessories etc.	Magazines	Date of loss*
Silver Cedar	4354	M.	British		not recorded	2000	in 210 cases		17-10-41
Aust	5630	S.	Norway	N.Y.	Bombay	4000	w/spares & accessories in 450 cases	48,000 box magazines	3-4-42
Tredinnick	4589	S.	British	N.Y.	Bombay	2500	w/spares & accessories in 282 cases.	30,000 box magazine	25-3-42
Empire Lotus	3683	S.	British			10 Mod 28AC in case G.47			week ending 16-5-42
Ardenvohr	5025	M.	British	USA	Australia	3249	w/spares & accessories in 200 cases.	32490 box magazine	10-6-42
ditto	5025	M.	British	USA	Australia	2000	w/spares & accessories in 200 cases.	21500 box magazine	10-6-42
West Ira	5681	S.	USA	N.Y.	Basra	1000	w/spares & accessories in 110 cases.	10,000 in 110 cases	21-6-42
Elmwood	7167	S.	USA	N.Y.	Basra	750	w/spares & accessories in 85 cases.	7500 box magazine in 75 cases	27-7-42
Maritima	5801	S.	British	N.Y.	U.K.		16 boxes 16 ¼ sets maintenance spare parts for TSMG STR1067K. 2 boxes 2 ½ maintenance spares for TSMG SR1067	78 cases 20rnd box	2-11-42 or 3-11-42
K.G. Meldhal	3799	S.	Norway	N.Y.	Bombay		13 cases spares	magazine	12-11-42
Empire Hawk	5033	S.	British	N.Y.	Alexandria	1000	w/spares & accessories in 109 cases.		12-12-42
Modavia	4858	M.	British	Canada	Southampton	2 cases 12 TSMG			27-2-43

Ship	Position Lost (B.R.1337)	Attacked by: (B.R.1337)	Cause of loss (B.R.1337)	Remarks	Additional information not in records (internet etc.)
Silver Cedar	53°36' N. 30°00' W.	S.M.	T.	true name 'Silvercedar'	torpedoed by U-553 in North Atlantic en route from New York and Sydney, C.B. for Liverpool in convoy SC-48
Aust	20° S. 16° W. (approx)	Raider			Sunk by German commerce raider Thor in South Atlantic en route from Brooklyn and St. Thomas via Brazil and Capetown for Bombay. Crew taken as prisoners to Japan. Position said to be 21° S. 16° W.
Tredinnick	27°15' N. 49°15'W. (approx.)	S.M.*		*presumed cause	Torpedoed by Italian submarine Pietro Calvi in mid-Atlantic
Empire Lotus	not in B.R. 1337				Foundered in bad weather off Nova Scotia 12-5-42 en route from New York and Halifax N.S. for Belfast
Ardenvohr	12°45' N. 80°20'W.	S.M.	T.		Torpedoed by U-68 off Nicaragua en route from New York and Hampton Roads for Panama, Sydney and Melbourne
ditto					ditto
West Ira	12°28' N. 57°05'W.	S.M.	T.		Torpedoed by U-128 120 miles S.E. of Barbados en route from New York for Table Bay, Bushir and Bandar Shahpur
Elmwood	04°48' N. 22° 00'W.	S.M.	T.		torpedoed by U-130 off West Africa en route from New York and Trinidad for Table Bay, Abadan and Kuwait
Maritima	52°20'N. 45°40W.	S.M.	T.		Torpedoed by U-552 500 miles W. of St. John's N.F. in convoy SC-107. Spelling also given as Maratima.
K.G. Meldhal	34°59' S., 29°45' E.	S.M.	T.	true spelling is Meldahl (B.R.1337)	Torpedoed by U-181 off Natal en route from New York and Port of Spain via Capetown for Bombay
Empire Hawk	05°56'N. 39°50W.	S.M.	T.		Sunk by Italian submarine Enrico Tazzoli off French Guiana
Modavia	090° 14 miles from Berry Head (Lyme Bay)	E-boat	T.		English coastal waters. Left Milford Haven for Portsmouth in convoy WP-300. Divers report wreck has been extensively salvaged.

Ship	G.T.	Type of propulsion	Flag	Port of Departure	Destination	No. of guns	Accessories etc.	Magazines	Date of loss*
Mariso	7659	S.	Dutch	N.Y.	Alexandria	4637 TSMG M1 .45cal	w/spares in 484 boxes	69555 magazines in 431 cases	20-3-43
ditto	7659	S.	Dutch	N.Y.	Alexandria	1000	w/spares in 105 boxes	15000 in 150 boxes	20-3-43
ditto	7659	S.	Dutch	N.Y.	Alexandria	200	w/spares in 21 boxes	3000 in 8 boxes	20-3-43
Agwimonte	6679	S.	USA	N.Y.	Suez		5 sets maintenance spares for TSMG in 8 boxes		28-5-43
Santos	4639	M.	Norway	USA	U.K.		1 box ½ set maintenance for .45 cal. TSMG for M4A4 Med. Tanks (OSO56350).		23-8-43
ditto	4639	M.	Norway	USA	U.K.		1 box ¼ set for .45 TSMG (OSO52296).		23-8-43
ditto	4639	M.	Norway	USA	U.K.		8 cases 2½ sets Spares & Accessories for .45 TSMG (OSO48439-48441)		23-8-43
ditto	4639	M.	Norway	USA	U.K.		3 boxes 1½ set and 1¾ set maintenance spares for .45 TSMG		23-8-43
ditto	4639	M.	Norway	USA	U.K.		14 cases cleaning equipment & gun slings for TSMG		23-8-43
ditto	4639	M.	Norway	USA	U.K.		1 box ½ set maintenance for .45 cal. TSMG for M4A4 Tanks (OS56351)		23-8-43
ditto	4639	M.	Norway	USA	U.K.		1 box ½ set maintenance for .45 cal. TSMG for M4A4 Tanks		23-8-43

Ship	Position Lost (B.R.1337)	Attacked by: (B.R.1337)	Cause of loss (B.R.1337)	Remarks	Additional information not in records (internet etc.)
Mariso	13°20' S. 37°25'W.	S.M.	T.		Torpedoed by U-518 90 nm off Bahia, Brazil en route from New York and Trinidad to Durban and Alexandria. Some of crew taken prisoner.
ditto	*ditto*	*ditto*	*ditto*		
ditto	*ditto*	*ditto*	*ditto*		
Agwimonte	34°57' S., 19°33' E.	S.M.	T.	Torpedoed again on 29th and sunk	Torpedoed by U-177 en route in convoy CD-20 to Durban and Saldanha Bay for Suez and sunk off Cape Agulhas, South Africa, 28-5-43
Santos	not in B.R. 1337			sunk by enemy action	In collision with S.S. Theodore Dwight Weld 18/19-8-43 and foundered S. of Newfoundland en route from N.Y. to Liverpool in convoy HX-252. Escort believed convoy was under attack. No German record of any attack on this convoy. Position approx. 43° 51' N. 53° 12' W.
ditto	*ditto*				*ditto*
ditto	*ditto*				*ditto*
ditto	*ditto*				*ditto*
ditto	*ditto*				*ditto*
ditto	*ditto*			additional manifest filed 5-9-43	*ditto*
ditto	*ditto*				*ditto*

Pre Lease Lend Requirements.

Thompson Guns.

Demand No	No Ordered	Cable Ordering	Date of Cable	Firm Producing	Quantity Delivered	Remarks
1. 0.0/218/1/600	750 1,340 55,250	/66	2.2.40	Auto Ordnance Co	750	5,12,71 Delivered 3,950 lost in Transit.
" 218/6/1049	1569	24.6.40	"	Completed.		
" 218/7/1297	17,000	Suply 729	17.9.40	"		
" 218/8/1323	27,000	" 923	3.10.40	"	26,000	1000 lost in Transit.
" 218/9/1570	50,000	" 1274	19.12.40	"		42,000 of This order now under ...

LEFT: An excerpt of the MoS table affixed to the inside cover of the file containing much of the information included in this book. This table has been reproduced in the Chapter Eleven for easy reference (p. 123).

Chapter Nine: The Thompson & the Irish Army

The use of the terms Great Britain, England and United Kingdom appear at times interchangeable. Such is not the case. Great Britain, a large island, is composed of three geographic regions: England (the largest region located in the South and includes the city of London, Scotland (also of great size and located to the North of England) and Wales (much smaller and located to the West of England). The citizenry of Wales and Scotland are not part of England; they are citizens of Great Britain or the United Kingdom.

The United Kingdom is presently composed of Great Britain and Northern Ireland. At one time the entire island of Ireland was part of the United Kingdom. In 1921, after an insurrection variously known as the 'Anglo-Irish war,' the 'Irish War of Independence,' the 'Tan War,' or simply 'The Troubles,' Ireland was partitioned into the Northern and Southern regions by an act of the British parliament. The next year twenty-six counties in the South became the Irish Free State, a separate country. The parliament of Northern Ireland, a much smaller region located in the north east part of the island, elected to remain part of the United Kingdom. The history of Ireland is way too vast and complex to detail in this book. However, it is important to point out the Thompson submachine gun is an important part of that history because it was the weapon of choice for the Irish Republican Army or I.R.A. for many years.

At the beginning of World War II the Irish Free State (by now known simply as Éire) decided to remain neutral during the hostilities. Given its close proximity to Great Britain, a state of neutrality proved difficult for Ireland. With the evacuation of British forces at Dunkirk in June 1940 and the fall of Paris shortly thereafter, the war in Europe became a reality. If Germany successfully invaded Great Britain it was possible that Ireland would be next. Several of the Northern Irish sea ports were key to the Battle of the Atlantic, at least in the early years. Some thought it possible that Great Britain might invade Ireland if the military situation required it. Irish military planners were tasked with defending possible German and/or British invasions. That said, the army of Ireland was never fully funded or staffed prior to the start of World War II. All types of weapons were in very short supply. During what was termed as "The Emergency" every type of firearm was put to use, including unserviceable Lee-Enfield "drill purpose" rifles and Brown Bess flintlock muskets originally issued circa 1798. [348]

An inventory of weapons of the Irish Army on March 31, 1940 revealed 21 caliber .450 "Thompson SMG." These would have been of Colt manufacture, most likely early Models of 1921 originally purchased and smuggled to Ireland by the I.R.A. Aside from the Thompson gun, the only other available submachine guns were 14 Bergmann 9mm SMGs. As the war progressed, the British War Office supplied 99 more Thompson guns during the 1942/43 time frame. Of note, three Thompson guns were "purchased locally" in 1943/44. And the Garda Síochána (national law enforcement agency) provided one Neuhausen 9mm SMG, also in 1943/44. The pedigree of these four weapons is unknown. Ammunition for all weapons, or the lack there of, was another continual problem for the Irish Army. However, the same March 1940 inventory indicated 1,459,916 rounds of .45 caliber ammunition in stock – more than enough to supply the original 21 Thompson guns. [349]

---

[348] Various authors, 'THE EMERGENCY' 1939-45, *The Irish Sword, Vol. XIX,* (1993-4, Nos. 75 &76), 19, 27, 47-50, 71
[349] Donal O'Carroll, "The emergency army," *The Irish Sword, Vol. XIX,* (1993-4, Nos. 75 &76) 36-38

from the Michael Curran collection, United Kingdom

An undated World War II photograph showing the use of the Thompson gun by an Irish solider at the Curragh Camp in Ireland. The photograph was taken later in the war as the soldiers are wearing British supplied helmets and uniforms. Note the absence of the compensator and improvised sling attachment. This is most likely one of the early Thompson guns originally purchased by the I.R.A. See close-up, below.

Chapter Ten: Pictures of the Thompson Gun

No story about the Thompson gun would be complete without pictures of this beautiful firearm. The first Thompson gun commercially manufactured was the Model of 1921. The production run by Colt's Patent Firearms Manufacturing Company, Hartford, Connecticut, began in 1921 and ended in 1922. The serial number of the first production Colt Thompson was number 41; the last serial number was 15040. These first 15,000 Model of 1921 guns composed the entire inventory of Auto-Ordnance Corporation for 19 years. All variations and different models of the Thompson gun offered for sale by Auto-Ordnance until 1940 were modifications of these original 15,000 guns. When the British government placed the first order for 750 Model 21A.C. Thompson guns, Auto-Ordnance officials quickly advised that production of the Model of 1921 had been discontinued. What they failed to mention was production of the Model of 1921 was discontinued in 1922. If not for the foresight of Russell Maguire to place this old design back into production before the last of the 15,000 original Colt guns were sold, this may have been the only production of the Thompson gun.

An original Model of 1921 Thompson gun with 50 round drum. The profile is recognized internationally. This original design was later referred to in Auto-Ordnance literature as the Model of 1921A.

An original Model of 1921 Thompson with 50 round drum and Cutts Compensator. When the Cutts Compensator became available as an option in 1926, this gun was referred to in Auto-Ordnance literature as the Model of 1921AC.

The information provided in this chapter is not intended to be inclusive of all the known details regarding the markings on all different models and variations of the Thompson guns. It should be used only as a general guide that will allow the enthusiast to identify the type and possible variation of a Thompson gun under observation. This information does focus on the early Savage Thompson as these first guns were the basis for, *"Great Britain - The Tommy Gun Story."*

from the Dermot Foley collection, Great Britain

Shown above and below are the left side receiver markings of an original Model of 1921 Thompson gun. This is a former Irish Republican Army (IRA) Thompson. Notice the 3 digit serial number has been defaced; a common occurrence on IRA Thompsons. This is one of the first Colt Thompsons manufactured in 1921 and has the early fire select markings - the arrows are pointing down. Compare the arrow markings with NO 4328 on the following page. Even with the honest wear and tear and the finish nearly gone, this early Colt Thompson would be the centerpiece of most collections. A close-up of the model nomenclature and the defaced serial number is featured below.

from the Dermot Foley collection, Great Britain

from the Dermot Foley collection, Great Britain

A right side view of the former Colt IRA Thompson with the defaced serial number revealing the heavily worn and barely visible New York address and patent date markings. Again, note the lack of finish, especially when compared to NO 4328, below. These two Colt Thompsons led much different lives!

from the Chuck Isern collection, USA

The left side receiver markings of a Model of 1928 US NAVY Thompson: NO 4328. Note the fire control arrows pointing to the right and left in this later gun as opposed to down in the early Colt Thompson featured above. The original purchaser of NO 4328 was the Nassau County Police Department, Long Island, New York.

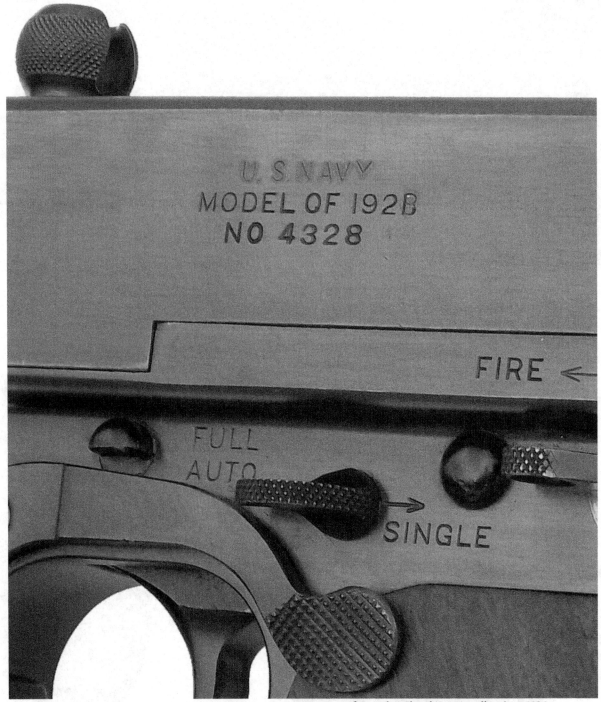

Close-up nomenclature markings on Colt manufactured Thompson NO 4328. Note how Auto-Ordnance has taken the letter 8 and handstamped it over the number 1 to create what looks like Model of 192B. The U.S. NAVY marking above the nomenclature is also handstamped. Notice the fine knurling on the actuator (cocking knob) and fire control levers and the near perfect coining on the end of the magazine catch.

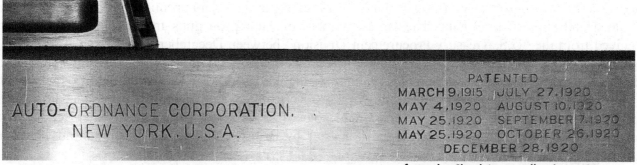

from the Chuck Isern collection, USA

The right side receiver markings on Model of 1928 US NAVY Thompson: NO 4328. Note how the Patent Date markings end with the year 1920. Colt Thompsons above the 14,500 serial number range end with Patent Date markings with the year 1922, same as on the first contract by Savage Arms for 10,000 guns. Also note how the *New York, U.S.A.* nomenclature is different from what is found on the early Savage Thompsons featured in the upcoming pages.

A common misconception among those who do not study the Thompson gun in detail is that thousands of Colt's manufactured Thompson guns were sold to the British government during World War II. This is simply not true. The number of Colt manufactured Thompsons purchased or even possessed by the British government at the beginning of World War II would have been negligible. Aside from a few captured IRA Thompsons, the only documented Colt manufactured guns in the British military were the six sent to the British Expeditionary Force in late 1939 and the two sent to the Director of Artillery in March 1940 by Auto-Ordnance for use in designing carrying chests. It is very likely the forty second-hand Thompson guns given to the British as part of a penalty in November 1940 when they assumed the French contract with Auto-Ordnance were "reconditioned" Colt guns. It is also possible some of the 3000 Colt manufactured Thompsons purchased by the French government in November 1939 could have found their way into British hands with the evacuations at Dunkirk and elsewhere. Likewise, there are several reports of Thompson guns going to Great Britain in the early days of the war outside of official government channels. Both instances involve the early formations of the clandestine Commando and Auxiliary Units. The first was a statement from Corporal Arthur Woodiwiss, 2 Commando, while at training at Inverlochy (Scotland). Corporal Woodiwiss stated, "I also remember that No. 2 received a present from the Mayor of New York, a chest full of tommy-guns confiscated from New York gangsters by the police. These went into our general weapon pool."[350] Next was a statement from Colonel Colin Gubbins (later Sir Colin) about the creation of the secretive Auxiliary Units in 1940 regarding his initial problems with the procurement of arms and equipment: "I received also a small windfall for our force from a friend in the United States, son of a former American ambassador here and a passionate anglophile, who had cabled me out the blue asking if he could help our country in any way, and I replied: pistols and sub-machine guns. A packing-case duly arrived at our HQ at Coleshill addressed simply to Colonel Gubbins, c/o The War Office, containing a couple of Thompsons and a nice selection of automatic pistols with ammunition to match."[351] These Thompson guns from America would certainly have been of Colt's manufacture.

The largest quantity of what was most likely Colt manufactured Thompsons was shipped to Britain by an organization named The American Committee for Defense of British Homes, based in New York City. It was a self-described "committee of American citizens seeking gifts of arms, ammunition, binoculars, steel helmets and stop-watches, from American civilians to be sent to the Civilian Committee for Defense of British Homes." Records from the American Committee revealed between its

[350] Robin Neillands, *The Raiders, The Army Commandoes 1940-1946* (London: Weidenfeld & Nicolson, 1989), 30
[351] Peter Wilkinson & Joan Bright Astley, *Gubbins and SOE* (London: Leo Cooper, 1993), 72

inception in September 1940 through June 3, 1942, some 110 Thompson submachine guns were obtained and shipped to Britain. The largest number of Thompson guns from a single source were received from the "U.S. Treasury Procurement Division" between December 8, 1941 and June 3, 1942 and consisted of 40 Thompsons "confiscated by Federal Agents." Of note is the following statement in their final report, "…only four shipments (compromising 35 cases) were lost at sea out of 64 shipments (compromising 795 cases). That is a loss rate of 4.4%, very similar to the loss rate experienced by all the Thompson gun shipments. [352] It is also conceivable other individual American owners could have donated a few more Thompsons as the call for arms by British civilians was heard and answered by American gun owners.

Regardless of the quantity, the facts indicate the number of Thompson guns manufactured by Colt's purchased, acquired, found, confiscated, or donated to the British military would have been extremely low and statistically insignificant.

Auto-Ordnance Corporation contracted with Savage Arms, Utica, New York, in December 1939 to manufacture 10,000 additional Thompson guns. No documentation has been found detailing the first serial number used by Savage. Those who study the Thompson believe the numbering started where the Colt's production ended – at 15041. Savage Thompson guns with serial numbers in the 15000 serial number range support this belief. A frame manufactured by Savage Arms exists with the serial number S-15043. [353] With the very few exceptions stated above, every Thompson gun purchased by the British government under cash and carry was of Savage manufacture. The very early Savage Thompsons were just about the same commercial quality of the Colt Thompsons, especially the ones sold to law enforcement agencies in the United States.

Photograph by Robert Segel, Pattern Room collection, Royal Armouries, Leeds
Model of 1928 Savage Thompson S-15960 with 30 round magazine. Note the sling swivel mounted on the right side of the vertical fore grip, a common British modification. A section of the barrel has been removed for some unknown reason. S-15960 is a very early Savage Thompson and may have been part of the first British order.

The lowest serial numbered Savage Thompson observed by author in the USA is S-15651. It would certainly have been part of the first order of 750 Thompson guns received by Great Britain in 1940 and put to use immediately. Another early Savage, S-15795, was last seen in England. A frame with serial number S-15832 has also been examined in the USA. The survival rate for Savage manufactured Thompson guns in the 15,000 serial number range appears to be very low. It is not hard to envision how most of these very early guns were simply used up and discarded or lost in battle.

---

[352] William B. Edwards, "The Disarmament of Great Britain, *American Rifleman*, January 1988, 69,70
[353] Tom Davis, Jr., "The Third Savage Thompson," *Small Arms Review*, September 2009, 42-47

MODEL OF 1928
NO. S- 15960

THOMPSON SUBMACHINE GUN
CALIBRE .45 AUTOMATIC CARTRIDGE

Left side receiver markings of Model of 1928 Thompson: S-15960. The "S" serial number prefix indicates this Thompson was manufactured by Savage Arms.

LEFT: Close-up of vertical fore grip on Savage S-15960 showing an Enfield offset sling swivel mounted on the right side of grip.

MODEL OF 1928
NO. S- 22802

THOMPSON SUBMACHINE GUN
CALIBRE .45 AUTOMATIC CARTRIDGE

FIRE ⟷ SAFE

Left side receiver markings of another early Model of 1928 Thompson: S-22802. Note the letter "S" serial number prefix indicating Savage Arms as the manufacturer.

MODEL OF 1928
NO. S-33791

THOMPSON SUBMACHINE GUN
CALIBRE .45 AUTOMATIC CARTRIDGE

FIRE ⟷ SAFE

The left side markings of another early Savage Thompson: S-33791.

from the Peter Ripley collection, Canada

Compare the different knurling pattern on the actuator (cocking knob) and fire control levers to commercially manufactured Colt Thompson NO 4328, above. The diamond design on the Colt era levers are pointed outward (like checkering); the diamonds on the early Savage levers are pointed inward. The knurling on the actuator and levers would later end as a cost cutting effort.

Savage Serial number S-167643, below, is from the Marc Siem collection, USA. This excellent picture highlights the left side receiver markings of a later Savage Thompson with US and A1 markings. Note the "TOMMY GUN" trademark and the Thompson signature in a bullet logo trademark on the top of the receiver. Also present are 1.) the GEG mark for George E. Goll, Auto-Ordnance Inspector, 2.) the RLB mark for Roy L. Bowlin, Army Inspector of Ordnance for the Rochester Ordnance District, and 3.) the Ordnance Department flaming bomb acceptance stamp. Note also how the fire control levers are not knurled and the magazine catch now features a hole in the middle of the knurling, unlike, Savage S-22802, above. The actuator or cocking knob still has the early knurling and S-167643 is equipped with the early milled flat ejector.

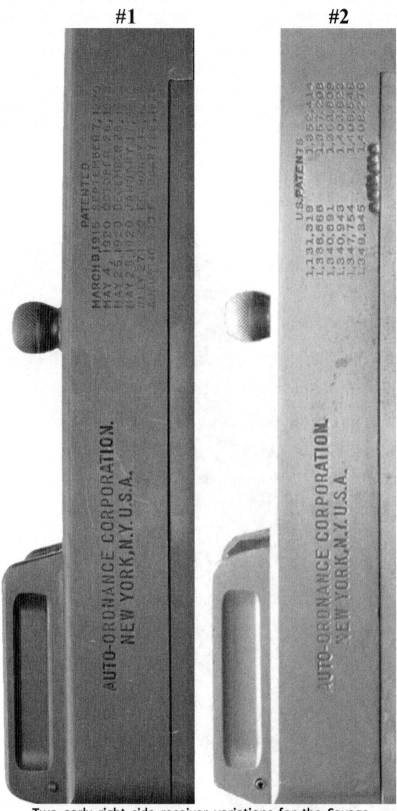

Two early right side receiver variations for the Savage manufactured Thompson submachine gun - numbered 1 and 2. Note the New York address and the patent <u>dates</u> and patent <u>numbers</u>.

#3   #4

Two later right side receiver variations for the
Savage manufactured Thompson submachine gun -
numbered 3 and 4. Note the Bridgeport, Connecticut
address and the different positioning of the address
and patent numbers.

There are four major receiver variations of Model 1928 Savage manufactured Thompson submachine guns. All four variations are pictured and numbered on the preceding two pages. The markings on the right side of the receivers are the key. The receiver marked #1 is from S-22802, above. Note the New York address and patent date markings ending in the year 1922. Patent date markings ending with the year 1922 were also marked on Colt manufactured Thompsons from serial number 14500 to 15040. Compare the New York address markings on this Savage Thompson to the New York address markings on Colt manufactured Thompson NO 4328, pictured on page 107. The highest numbered Savage receiver found by the author to date with a New York address and patent <u>dates</u> is S-25688.

The receiver marked #2, is from S-33791, above. Note the New York address and the patent numbers. The lowest numbered Savage receiver found by the author to date with a New York address and patent <u>numbers</u> is S-26732. Somewhere between serial numbers S-25688 and S-26732, the patent date receiver markings were changed to patent numbers. No exceptions to this research have been observed. If Savage began serial numbering receivers in the 15,000 serial number range as most experts believe, then patent dates were used on approximately the first 10,000 guns or the first order. These observations by the author are based on physical examinations and pictures of actual guns. The right side receiver of S-33791 also has what appears to be a depot repair to the receiver underneath the patent numbers. A series of punch marks are readily visible. It is unknown by whom, when or why this "repair" was performed.

The highest serial number observed by the author with a New York address and patent number markings is S-79878. Based on the dates of gun orders, known deliveries and production totals coupled with observed serial numbers and markings, it is very unlikely any Thompson guns provided to Great Britain under the Lend-Lease Act would have a New York address.

The receiver marked #3, is serial number S-85767; it is from the John Walsh collection, USA. Note the Bridgeport, Connecticut address. The lowest serial number on a Savage Thompson observed with the Bridgeport, Connecticut address is S-82240. However, a 1942 US Army Training film features an instructional cutaway of a 1928A1 Thompson, serial number S-81492, that too has a Bridgeport address.[354] Somewhere between S-79878 and S-81492, the New York address changed to the Bridgeport address. What makes this receiver variation unique is the positioning of the Bridgeport address and patent numbers. While the placement of the address and patent information mirrors what is found on receivers #1 and #2, above, this positioning appears to have only been used in the 80,000 and 90,000 serial number range – but research continues.

The receiver marked #4, is from S-167643, above. Note how the Bridgeport address is positioned toward the front of the receiver and patent numbers are positioned toward the end of the receiver under the rear sight assembly. This is the most common right side receiver variation for Model 1928 Thompson guns manufactured by Savage Arms. Aside from font changes and spacing, it is also the same basic right side receiver markings and positioning for Model 1928 Thompson receivers manufactured at the Auto-Ordnance Corporation plant at Bridgeport, Connecticut.

---

[354] Iannamico, 214

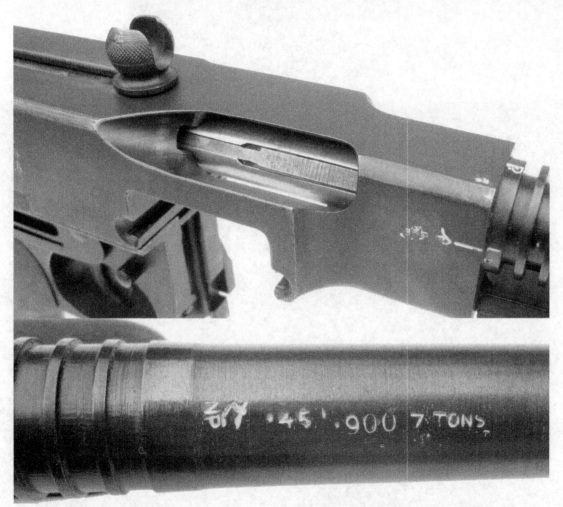

AUTO-ORDNANCE CORPORATION,
NEW YORK, N.Y. U.S.A.

MPD
509

PATENTED

MARCH 9, 1915   SEPTEMBER 7, 1920
MAY 4, 1920   OCTOBER 26, 1920
MAY 25, 1920   DECEMBER 25, 1920
MAY 25, 1920   JANUARY 17, 1922
JULY 27, 1920   FEBRUARY 14, 1922
AUGUST 10, 1920 FEBRUARY 28, 1922

from the Bob Devenney collection, USA

The above receiver displays the right side markings another early Savage Thompson: S-16863. Note the New York address and patent date markings ending in the year 1922. S-16863 is what collectors in the USA refer to as a *Savage Commercial Thompson*. Auto-Ordnance Corporation sold this early Savage Thompson to a law enforcement organization in the United States during World War II. The "MPD 509" markings were applied by the law enforcement organization. It is one of the rare instances where markings on a gun not applied at the factory (if tastefully done) actually increase the value of a gun.

.45 .900 7 TONS

from the Marc Siem collection, USA

Shown are some of the British proof markings found on S-167643. This is an excellent example of a US marked Savage Thompson that was mostly likely supplied to Great Britain under the Lend-Lease Act and later found its way back to the USA. The markings on the barrel are commercial London proof marks applied post military service and do not in themselves imply government ownership.

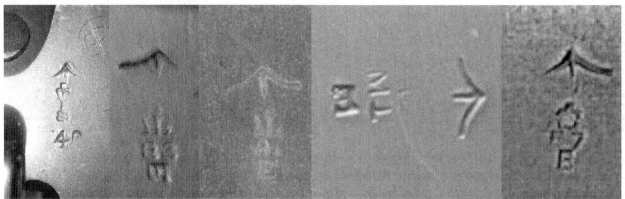

A collage of British markings found on early Savage manufactured Thompson guns, most likely indicating a cash and carry purchase. Note the Broad Arrow mark denoting government ownership is present on each gun.

from the Chuck Isern collection, USA
The patent date and AOC markings from the right side of the receiver of S-334906.

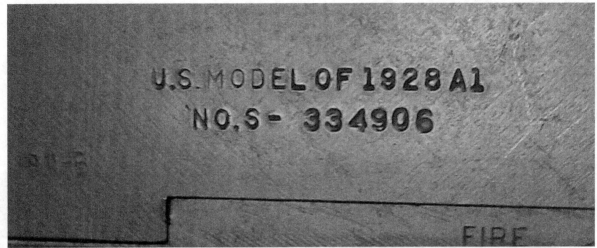

from the Chuck Isern collection, USA

The serial number and nomenclature markings on the left side of a later Savage Thompson, S-334906. Note the Army Inspector of Ordnance marking, "RLB," to the left of the serial number.

General Thompson formed Auto-Ordnance Corporation in 1916. Twenty-five years later Auto-Ordnance finally manufactured the first Thompson submachine gun in its own factory. There were two manufacturers of Thompson guns during World War II. Savage Arms in Utica, New York, as pictured earlier, and Auto-Ordnance Corporation at Bridgeport, Connecticut, commonly referred to as Auto-Ordnance Bridgeport (AOB). How do you tell the difference between a Savage and AOB Model of 1928 Thompson gun? Answer: the serial number. Savage guns will have an "S" prefix before the numbers; AOB guns will have an "AO" prefix before the numbers. These prefixes become part of the serial number thus avoiding duplicate serial numbers as most large customers, i.e., US military, British military, received Thompson guns from both manufacturing facilities. Like the Savage guns, there is no documentation that indicates what serial number Auto-Ordnance Bridgeport (AOB) used when production began. Based on when the AOB plant started production, all AOB Thompson guns supplied to British forces would have been under the Lend-Lease Act.

from the Ross Opsahl collection, USA

Typical butt stock modifications and repairs by British armourers: two re-enforcement screws and repair of two cracks in front of stock along with repositioning of the sling swivel from bottom of stock to top.

from the Dermot Foley collection, Great Britain

Serial number AO 10414, pictured above, is an excellent example of a very early AOB Thompson gun. The worn finish suggests heavy use. Note the two screws in the butt stock. This was a common British procedure to re-inforce the strength of butt stock. Note the lack of knurling on the fire control levers and actuator and the hole in the magazine catch flat pad. The ejector on this Thompson is one of the later stamped versions. Note the visible bump in it compared to the milled ejectors for on the Colt and early Savage Thompsons pictured above.

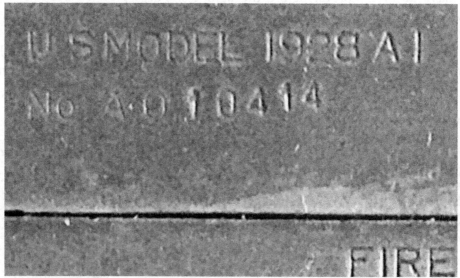

from the Dermot Foley collection, Great Britain

The serial number nomenclature of an Auto-Ordnance Bridgeport Thompson gun. Note the how the letter "o" in the "No" marking is smaller as opposed to the Colt and Savage guns, above. Using the "AO" serial number prefix, the serial number of this Thompson is A0 10414. This is the lowest serial numbered AOB gun observed by the author.

118

Close-up picture of the "THOMPSON SUBMACHINE" markings from AO 10414.

from the Peter Ripley collection, Canada

AO 93890 is a much later manufactured Auto-Ordnance Bridgeport Thompson gun. Note the "Full Auto" markings are in a straight line compared to the staggered markings on the Colt and Savage Thompsons pictured above. The "W.B." marking indicates Waldemar Broberg, Army Inspector of Ordnance for the Springfield Ordnance District. Below the W.B. mark is an Ordnance stamp in the shape of a wheel and crossed cannons. Both of these markings are common on AOB manufactured Thompson guns.

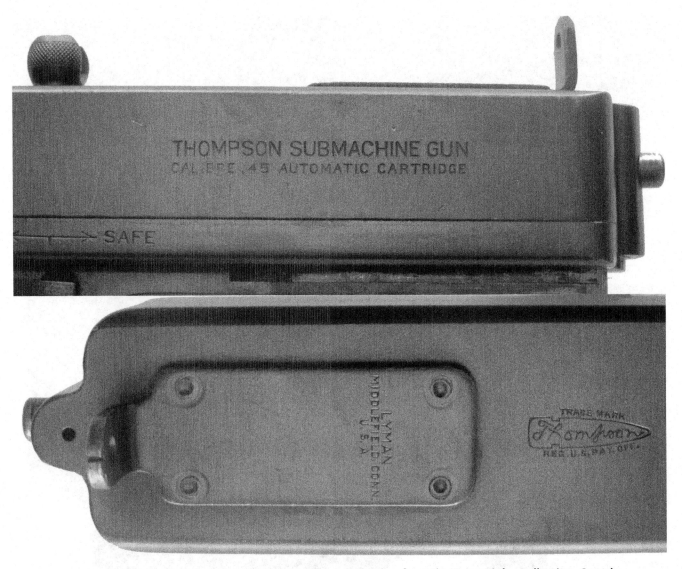

AO 93890 is in much better condition than AO10414, above. It still retains a knurled actuator. Of interest is the "new" L type rear sight, a cost cutting measure on all Thompson guns (p. 40). The LYMAN name and address markings on the rear sight indicate it is the first variation of the L sight. Later variations did not have the address markings. Also note the Thompson trademark name and bullet logo.

As the war progressed and the need for more Thompson guns increased, engineers at Savage Arms decided to simplify this very expensive piece of machinery. The end result was the M1 Thompson, soon to be the M1A1 Thompson. Gone were the removable butt stock, finned barrel, compensator and slots for the drum magazine. The complicated locking system highlighted by AOC in the early years as a great invention was changed to a simple blow-back design. All vestiges of the gangster look were eliminated when the cocking knob was moved to the right side of the receiver. Shown on the following page are the M1 (left) and M1A1 (right) Thompson submachine guns. Note the plain fixed L sight on the early M1 Thompson, later replaced by a fixed rear sight with side protectors.

from The American Thompson Reference Collection, USA

Chapter Eleven: Tables

The following tables have been created and/or reproduced from information compiled and used by the Ministry of Supply (MoS) during World War II. The tables are provided to assist the reader in understanding the information discussed throughout the story.

I.   Pre-Lease Lend Requirements. Thompson gun. Table found on inside cover of folder containing the bulk of the information discussed in the story.

II.   Initial or Immediate War Orders (IWO), primarily for guns

III.   INITIAL SPARES LIST (per five guns)

IV.   SPARES - SCHEDULE OF ANCILLARY ITEMS AND SPARES FOR 100 CARBINES MACHINE THOMPSON .45" PLUS REQUIREMENTS FOR 12MONTHS MAINTENANCE

V.   SPARES - W.S. 14 PROVISION SCHEDULE NO. 9

VI.   SPARES – REVISED W.S. 14 PROVISION SCHEDULE NO. 9A

VII.   SPARES - U.S.A. Ordnance Scale

I.

Demand No.	No Ordered	Cable Ordering	Date of Cable	Firm Producing	Quantity Delivered	Remarks
Pre Lease Lend Requirements. **Thompson Guns**						
0.0/218/1/600	750	166	2.2.40	Auto Ordnance Co	750	
	1,340			**French Ct take over**		
218/6/1049	55,250	1569	24.6.40	"	Completed	51271 Delivered 3,950 Lost in Transit
218/7/1297	17,000	Suply 729	17.9.40	"		
218/8/1323	27,000	" 923		"	26,000	1,000 Lost in Transit
* 218/9/1570	50,000	" 1274		"		* **42,000 of this order now under L.L.**

NOTE: The 1,340 Thompson guns from the French contract take over remark, above, appeared to be penciled into the table at a later date.

II.

Initial or Immediate War Orders (IWO) primarily for guns				
GUN ORDERS BY NUMBER	**IWO ISSUE NUMBER**	**DATES OF IWO's**	**AMOUNT OF GUNS ORDERED**	**ADDITIONAL INFORMATION**
1st	218/1	1-Feb-40	750	counted twice in MoS Ledger Book
2nd	218/5	14-May-40	2,000	cancelled with IWO for orders 3 & 4, see below
3rd*			26,250	includes 2nd order for 2000 guns & 1st order for 750 guns (mistake)
4th*	218/6	27-May-40	26,250	IWO total is for 55,250 Thompson guns (750 + 2000 + 26250 + 26250)
5th	218/7	19-Sep-40	17,000	
6th	218/8	8-Oct-40	27,000	originally ordered without compensators
7th		**NONE**, A-2308	54,000	not counted or referenced in MoS Ledger Book; No IWO issued
8th	218/9	17-Jan-41	50,000	
9th	218/10	9-Jun-41	158,000	
9th (Amended)	Special	9-Jun-41	6,000	Amended IWO "381/9 Special" for 6000 Programme B guns
10th	218/11	12-Aug-41	50,000	Amended on 18 Sep 1941 to include 575,000 box magazines
11th	218/12	25-Sep-41	150,000	Notation: "Instructions on spares will follow"
			567,250	TOTAL
			(54,000)	minus the 7th order of 54,000 guns from total
			513,250	
			750	plus 1st order for 750 guns counted twice in IWO for 55,250 guns, above
			514,000	TOTAL - Matches MoS Ledger Book

*One IWO was issued for the 3rd & 4th orders. This IWO specifically cancelled the IWO for the second IWO and added that 2000 gun order into the 55,250 gun total. However, it also added into the total the first order of 750 guns and did not cancel the first IWO.

Note the following IWO's for other than guns:

218/2 - Ammunition for Thompson Sub-Machine Guns (later changed to 218/A/1)
218/3 - Thompson Sub-Machine Gun. Spares
218/4 - Thompson Sub. Machine Gun Magazines
218/13 - Thompson Sub-Machine Gun 50 rounds Drum Magazines

III.

Initial Spares List	
for every five guns	
Barrels	1
Hammers	1
Recoil Springs	1
Extractors	5
Firing Pins	3
Firing Pin Springs	3
Hammer Pins	3
Gear [sic] Springs	3
Gear [sic] Lever Springs	3
Trigger Springs	3
Short Handle Breech Cleaning Brush	6
Later (1/12/40):	
Spring, Disconnector	5

IV.

		Quantity					
Cat. Nos.	Designation	Ancillary Items	for Unit	for Mtce	TOTAL	Remarks	Manufactured in U.K. = X*
B.D. 4041	Butts stock (stripped)			5	5		
B.D. 4042	Butts stock slide			5	5		
B.D. 4043	Butts Stock catch			5	5		
B.D. 4044	Butts stock catch button			5	5		
B.D. 4045	Butts Stock catch pin			5	5		
B.D. 4046	Butts Stock catch spring			5	5		
B.D. 4047	Butts stock screw gauge			5	5		
B.D. 4048	Butts stock screw washer			5	5		
B.D. 4049	Butts plate (stripped)			5	5		
B.D. 4050	Butts plate cap			5	5		
B.D. 4051	Butts plate pin			5	5		
B.D. 4052	Butts plate spring			5	5		
B.D. 4053	Butts plate spring screw			5	5		
B.D. 4054	Butts plate screw large			5	5		
B.D. 4055	Butts plate screw small			5	5		
B.D. 4056	Receiver			5	5		
B.D. 4057	Bracket and swivel butt			5	5		
B.E.							
B.E. 9994	Rod Cleaning	100		5	105		
B.E. 4030	Rod Cleaning wire brush	100		5	105		X
B.E. 9974	Brush Breech bristle	100	50	5	155		
B.E. 9999	Oil Can (in butt)	100			100		
B.E. 4000	Axis, sear and trigger			5	5		
B.E. 9973	Barrels			10	10		
B.E. 4001	Blocks breech			3	3		
B.E. 4002	Catches Magazine			2	2		
B.E. 4003	Discs buffer (fibre)			10	10		
B.E. 4004	Ejectors			3	3		
B.E. 9975	Extractors		20	10	30		

SCHEDULE OF ANCILLARY ITEMS AND SPARES FOR 100 CARBINES MACHINE THOMPSON .45" PLUS REQUIREMENTS FOR 12 MONTHS MAINTENANCE

B.E. 4005	Grips fore		3	3
B.E. 4006	Grips pistol		3	3
B.E. 4007	Guards trigger		0.5	0.5
B.E. 4008	Handles cocking		1	1
B.E. 9981	Levers pin firing	10	3	13
B.E. 4009	Levers, safety		1	1
B.E. 4010	Levers sear		1	1
B.E. 4011	Levers trigger		2	2
B.E. 4012	Levers trip		2	2
B.E. 4013	Locking pieces		2	2
B.E. 4014	Oilers, breech		10	10
B.E. 9977	Pins, firing	10	5	15
B.E. 9980	Pins lever pin firing	10	3	13
B.E. 4015	Pin lever trip		2	2
B.E. 4016	Plates fore grip		1	1
B.E. 4017	Plungers guard trigger		5	5
B.E. 4018	Rods spring return		2	2
B.E. 4019	Screws grip fore		3	3
B.E. 4020	Screws grip pistol		3	3
B.E. 4021	Sears		1	1
B.E. 4022	Springs catch magazine		5	5
B.E. 9983	Springs lever sear	10	5	15
B.E. 4023	Springs lever trigger		5	5
B.E. 9978	Springs pin firing	10	10	20
B.E. 4024	Springs plunger guard trigger		5	5
B.E. 9982	Springs recoil	20	20	40
B.E. 9984	Springs sear	10	5	15
B.E. 9985	Springs trigger	10	5	15
B.E. 4025	Triggers		1	1
B.E. 4026	Trips		2	2
B.E. 4027	Butts (complete)		5	5
B.E. 4028	Compensators		2	2
B.E. 4029	Leaves backsight		5	5
B.E. 4030	Pins compensator		2	2
B.E. 4031	Pins leaf backsight		2	2
B.E. 4032	Plungers backsight		2	2
B.E. 4033	Slides leaf backsight (complete)		5	5

B.E. 4034	Springs catch butt			5	5	
B.E. 4035	Springs plunger backsight			5	5	
B.E. 4036	Bottles oil			5	5	X
~~B.E. 9974~~	~~Breech cleaning brush~~	~~100~~		~~5~~	~~105~~	
B.E. 9986	Tools assembly recoil spring	100		5	105	X
	Handbooks	100			100	
	Magazines 20-rd.	1,000	150	5	1155	
B.B.						
B.B. 520	Pullthroughs Cord single	100		5	105	X
B.B. 521	Gauze pieces	100		5	105	X
B.B. 522	Weights	100		5	105	X

* Minute Sheet No. 1 to M.P.F. from A.D.W.S. , dated July 19th 1941

NOTE: Cat. Nos. are the catalog numbers in the (British) Vocabulary of Army Ordnance Stores

NOTE: B.E. 9999 Oil Can (in butt) - this is believed to be the commonly found AOC supplied black-crackle painted oil can

NOTE: B.E. 4036 Bottles oil - this is believed to be the standard Lee-Enfield oil bottle

V.

W.S. 14 PROVISION SCHEDULE NO. 9						
SCHEDULE OF ANCILLIARY ITEMS, TOOL, SPARES FOR 100 CARBINES MACHINE THOMPSON PLUS ITEMS REQUIRED FOR 12 MONTHS MAINTENANCE						
1	2	3	4	5	6	7
		Quantity				
Cat.No.	Designation	Ancill-ary Items	Unit Spares	for mtcs	Total	Remarks
B.E.	Carbines, Machine, Thompson .45" : -					
B.E. 4028	Cutts Compensator	100		2	102	
~~B.E. 4030~~	~~Rod Cleaning wire brush~~	~~100~~		~~50~~	~~150~~	
~~B.E. 4039~~	~~Rods Cleaning~~					
~~B.E. 9997~~	~~Brush~~					
~~B.E. 9995~~	~~wire~~			~~80~~	~~80~~	
~~B.E. 9996~~	~~bristle~~			~~80~~	~~80~~	
	~~Adaptors~~			~~80~~	~~80~~	
	~~Loops~~			~~80~~	~~80~~	
B.E. 9974	Breech brush bristle	100	50	80	230	
B.E. 9999	Cans Oil	100		80	180	
	Magazines Thompson Carbine .45"					
	Box Type	1,000	150	5	1,155	
	Platform			5	5	
	Plate Bottom			5	5	
	Spring			10	10	
	Carbines, Machine, Thompson .45" : -					
B.E. 4000	Axis, Sear and Trigger			5	5	
B.E. 9973	Barrels			10	10	
B.E. 4001	Blocks breech			3	3	
B.E. 4002	Catches, Magazine			2	3	
B.E. 4003	Disks, Buffer (fibre)			10	10	
B.E. 4004	Ejectors			3	3	
B.E. 9975	Extractors		20	10	30	
B.E. 4005	Grips, fore			3	3	
B.E. 4006	Grips, pistol			3	3	
B.E. 4007	Guards, trigger			0.5	0.5	
B.E. 4008	Handles, cocking			1	1	
B.E. 9981	Levers, pin, firing			3	3	

129

B.E. 4009	Levers, safety		1	1
B.E. 4010	Levers, sear		1	1
	Carbines, Machine, Thompson .45" : -			
B.E. 4011	Levers, trigger		2	2
B.E. 4012	Levers, trip		2	2
B.E. 4013	Locking, pieces		2	2
B.E. 4014	Oilers, breech		10	10
B.E. 9997	Pins, firing	10	5	15
B.E. 9980	Pins, lever, firing pin	10	5	15
B.E. 4015	Pins, lever, trip		2	2
B.E. 4016	Plates, fore, grip		1	1
B.E. 4017	Plungers, guard, trigger		5	5
B.E. 4019	Rods, spring, return		2	2
B.E. 4018	Screws, grip, fore		3	3
B.E. 4020	Screws, grip, pistol		3	3
B.E. 4021	Sears		1	1
B.E. 4022	Springs, catch, magazine		5	5
B.E. 9983	Springs, lever, sear	10	5	15
B.E. 4023	Springs, lever, trigger		5	5
B.E. 9978	Springs, pin, firing	10	10	20
B.E. 4024	Springs, plunger, guard, trigger		5	5
B.E. 9982	Springs, recoil	20	20	40
B.E. 9984	Springs, sear	10	5	15
B.E. 9985	Springs, trigger		5	5
B.E. 4025	Trigger	10	1	11
B.E. 4026	Trips		2	2
B.E. 4027	Butts (complete)		5	5
B.E. 4029	Leaves, backsight		5	5
B.E. 4030	Pins, compensator		2	2
B.E. 4031	Pins, leaf, backsight		2	2
B.E. 4032	Plungers, backsight		2	2
	Carbines, Machine, Thompson .45" : -			
B.E. 4033	Sides, leaf backsight (complete)		5	5
B.E. 4034	Springs, catch, butt		5	5
B.E. 4035	Springs, plunger, backsight		5	5
B.E. 4036	Bottles, oil, Mk. IV or Mk.V.		10	10

Note: Unit Spares are based on requirement of 10 weapons
viz. 1/10th of Co. 4
Authority : 57/Gen./1541.

130

VI.

CYPHER TELEGRAM

To the B.P.C. and B.A.D. Washington. From the W.O. and Min. of Supply.

Sent 2.0 p.m. 1st February 1942

SUMIL .73

Immediate.

Milau 45

Revised W.S.14 No.9A schedule for Thompson Machine Carbine given below.

(A) shows designation
(B) U.S.A. part number
(C) Users consumption per centage in M.E. [Middle East] for one year based on 100 weapons
(D) W.S. 14 Schedule No.9A Proposed scale 100 Equipments for 12 months

A.	B.	C.	D.
Actuator	18A	Nil	2/5
Barrels	1A	3/10	6
Bolts	11A	1/2	1
Caps Butt plate	34C	Nil	Recover
Catches Butt stock with Button	32B&G	Nil	Recover
Catches Magazine with pin	7 B&C	Nil	1/5
Catches rear sight slide assembled	37G	Nil	See Note A
Collars, windage screw	37 C	Nil	Nil
Compensator, recoil (Cutts)	39 A	Nil	Recover
Disconnectors	6 D	1/20	2/5
Ejectors	4 B	3/10	1
Extractors	15 A	5	8
Eyepieces	36 F	Nil	Recover
Frames	5A	3/20	Recover
Grips, fore	17 D	1/2	1
Grips, rear	13 B	Nil	1
Hammers	14 B	1/10	2/5
Latches, frame	4 D	Nil	2/5
Leaves, rear sight, assembled	36 B	Nil	See Note A
Levers, sear	16 A	Nil	2/5
Locks	3 A	1/5	2/5
Mounts, grip	7 G	Nil	Recover
Oiler, breech, with pad	8 A&B	1/2	1
Pads, buffer	17 B	Nil	1
Pilots, buffer	17 A	5/10	4/5
Pins, Butt plate	34 E	Nil	Recover
Pins, Butt stock catch	32 E	Nil	Recover
Pins, firing	14 A	5	6
Pin, front sight	35 B	Nil	Recover
Pins, hammer	14 B	2/5	2/5
Pins, sight base	36 A	Nil	2/5
Pins, stop, rear sight slide	36 G	Nil	See Note A
Pivots, rocker	16 C	Nil	Nil
Plate, butt with bracket & 2 rivets	34A&B & F	Nil	Recover

Plates Butt Assembled	Nil	Nil	Recover
Plates, pivot	7 K	3/10	1/2
Plungers, rear sight leaf	37 M	Nil	See Note A
Receivers assembled	2 A	Nil	Recover
Rockers	16 D	Nil	2/5
Safety	7 A	Nil	2/5
Screws, butt plate, large	34 G	Nil	Recover
Screws, butt plate, small	34 F	Nil	Recover
Screws, butt plate, spring	34 J	Nil	Recover
Screws, butt stock, large	32D	Nil	Recover
Screws, butt stock, small	32C	Nil	Recover
Screws, fore grip	17E	Nil	2/5
Screws, rear grip	13D	Nil	2/5
Screws, rear sight slide catch	37H	Nil	See Note A
Sears	6 A	3/10	4/5
Sights front	39B	Nil	Recover
Slides, Butt stock	32A	Nil	Recover
Slides, rear sight	36C	Nil	See Note A
Springs, Butt plate	34D	Nil	Recover
Springs, Butt stock catch	32H	Nil	2/5
Springs, disconnector	9 A	2/5	2/5
Springs, firing pin	14C	3	4
Springs, frame latch	9 F	2/5	2/5
Springs, Magazine catch	9 D	3/20	2/5
Springs, rear sight plunger	37F	Nil	See Note A
Springs, recoil	17C	15	12
Springs, sear	9 B	2 3/4	2
Springs, sear lever	16 B	2 1/2	4
Springs, trigger	9 C	1/2	1
Stocks, assembled	Nil	1 1/2	2
Stocks, Butt	33 A	1/10	1/5
Swivels slings with plate and screw	21A and 23A	Nil	Recover
Triggers	6 C	1/20	Recover
Trips	6 B	1/10	2/5
Washers, Butt stock screw	32 F	Nil	Recover
Magazines 20 rnds box type	Nil	Nil	10
Followers Magazine 19	19 B	Nil	10
Plates Floor	19 A	Nil	10
Springs Magazine	19 C	Nil	10
Tubes Magazine	Nil	Nil	10
Oilers sub-machine gun	Nil	Nil	10
Brushes chamber cleaning M6	Nil	Nil	20

(CYPHER)

Note. A. Not required as future supplies of carbines will be fitted with aperture backsight.

Emphasis should be placed on items shown as "Recover". User experience shows nil requirements.

Recover in Column D, indicates that those items should be received from unrepairable weapons.

Originated - W.S. 14 W.O.
Agreed - P.A.S.(P) M.O.S.

W.O. Distribution: D.D.S.D. (W) D.D.W.S. (A) D.G.A.R. Q(OS) 4,
N.A.S. A.R.1. (b) A.C.I.G.S., S.D.1c. 12, W.S.14.

VII.

Part No. (Piece Mark or Stock No.)	Drawing No	Designation (list of parts) U.S.A. Designations (with British designations in brackets)	Per 100 Equipments			Total U.S. Schedule No.	Remarks
			Orgn. Spares (Unit plus Field Parks)	12 Mths Maint.	Total		
18A	45-G-22	Actuator (Handles cocking)		23	23		
1A	45-1-1	Barrel		120	120		
11A	45-1-13	Bolt (Blocks breech)		35	35		
	45-6-2	Catch butt stock assembly		10	10		one 32B and one 32G
7H	45-1-7	Catch magazine assembly (composed of:-		30	30		
7B		One 45-1-7 magazine catch (1)					
7C		One 45-1-7 magazine catch PIN (1)					
37G	45-7-3	Catch, rear sight slide assembly (composed of:-		43	43		
37K		One 45-7-3 rear sight slide catch SPRING (1)					
37L		one 45-7-3 rear sight slide catch STUD (1)					
37C	45-7-3	collar, windage screw		35	35		
39A		Compensator, recoil (cutts) (Cutts compensator)		3	3		
6D	45-1-6	Disconnector (Lever trigger)	100	50	150		
4B	45-G-4	Ejector	100	50	150		
15A	45-1-17	Extractor	100	50	150		
36F	45-7-2	Eyepiece		23	23		
17D	45-1-24	Grip, fore, horizontal		35	35		
13B	45-1-24	Grip, rear, vertical (Grip pistol)		35	35		
14B	45-1-16	Hammer (Lever pin firing)		35	35		
4D	45-G-4	Latch, frame (Plunger guard trigger)		43	43		
36B	45-7-2	Leaf, rear sight (Leaf back sight)		5	5		
		Leaf, rear sight, assembly (composed of:-		23	23		
36F		one eyepiece					
36B		one rear sight leaf					
36C		one rear sight slide					
37G		one rear sight slide catch, assembly					
37H		one rear sight slide catch, screw					
36G		one rear sight slide stop pin					
37D		one windage screw					
37C		one windage collar					
37E		one windage screw collar pin.)					
16A	45-1-18	Lever, sear		30	30		
3A	45-1-3	Lock (Locking pieces)		23	23		
		Magazine, 20 rounds					see scale accessories
		Magazine, 50 rounds					see scale accessories
7G	45-1-7	Mount, grip (Plates fore grip)		2	2		

		Oiler, breech, assembly (composed of:-		58	58
8A	45-1-8	One 45-1-8 breech oiler (1)			
8B		one 45-1-8 breech oiler pad (2)			
17B	45-1-21	Pad, buffer (Disc buffer (fibre))		35	35
17A	45-1-21	Pilot, buffer (Rods spring return)		23	23
34E	45-6-4	Pin, butt plate		5	5
32E	45-6-2	Pin, butt stock catch		5	5
14A	45-1-16	Pin, firing	100	50	150
35B	45-7-1	Pin, front sight (Pin compensator)		3	3
14B	45-1-16	Pin, hammer (Pin lever pin firing)		35	35
36A	45-7-2	Pin, sight base (Pin leaf back sight)		23	23
36G	45-7-2	Pin, stop, rear sight slide		35	35
37E	45-7-3	Pin, windage, screw collar		5	5
16C	45-1-18	Pivot, rocker (Lever trip)		35	35
		Plate, butt w/cap assembly (Composed of:-		23	23
		one butt Plate (composed of 34F, 34A, 34B)			
34C		One 45-6-4 butt plate cap			
34E		One 45-6-4 butt plate pin			
34D		One 45-6-4 butt plate Spring			
34J		One 45-6-4 butt plate spring screw			
7K	45-1-7	Plate, pivot, assembly (axis sear and trigger) (Composed of:-		43	43
7F		One 45-1-8 pivot Plate (1)			
7D		one 45-1-7 sear Pivot (1)			
7E		one 45-1-7 trigger Pivot (1)			
37M	45-7-3	Plunger, rear sight leaf assembly (Plunger back sight) (Composed of:		23	23
37A		one 45-7-3 sight Plunger (1)			
		one 45-7-3 sight Plunger Pin (1)			
28B	45-5-10	Retainer, rotor		70	70
16D	45-1-18	Rocker (Lever trip)	100	50	150
7A	45-1-7	Safety (Lever safety)		35	35
34G	45-6-4	Screw, butt plate, large		30	30
34H	45-6-4	Screw, butt plate, small		30	30
34J	45-6-4	Screw, butt plate, spring		5	5
32D	45-6-2	Screw, butt stock, large		23	23
32C	45-6-2	Screw, butt stock, small		23	23
17E	45-1-24	Screw, fore grip (Screws grip fore)		23	23
13D	45-1-15	Screw, rear grip (Screws grip pistol)		23	23
37H	45-7-3	Screw, rear sight slide catch		30	30
		Screw, sling swivel plate		58	58
37D	45-7-3	Screw, windage		5	5
6A	45-1-6	Sear		43	43
36C	45-7-2	Slide, rear sight		23	23
9A	45-1-9	Spring, disconnector (Spring lever trigger)	100	50	150
14C	45-1-16	Spring, firing pin (Spring pin firing)	100	50	150
9F	45-1-9	Spring, frame latch (Spring plunger guard trigger)		70	70

9D	45-1-9	Spring, magazine catch (Spring catch magazine)	100	50	150	
37F	45-7-3	Spring, rear sight plunger (Spring plunger back sight)		40	40	
17C	45-1-21	Spring, recoil (Spring recoil)	100	50	150	
9B	45-1-9	Spring, sear (Spring sear)	100	50	150	
16B	45-1-18	Spring, sear lever (Spring lever sear)		50	50	
9C	45-1-9	Spring, trigger (Spring trigger)		50	50	
		Stock, assembly (Butt complete) (Composed of:-		12	12	
		one butt plate, wcap assem.				
34G		one 45-6-4 butt plate screw, large				
34H		one 45-6-4 butt plate screw, small				
33A		one 45-6-3 butt stock				
		one butt stock catch, assem.				
32E		one 45-6-2 butt stock catch, pin				
32H		one 45-6-2 butt stock catch spring				
32D		one 45-6-2 butt stock catch screw, large				
32C		one 45-6-2 butt stock catch screw, small				
32F		two 45-6-2 butt stock screw washer				
32A		one 45-6-2 butt stock slide				
21C		two 45-1-24 sling swivel plate screw)				
33A	45-6-3	Stock, butt, swivel, sling assembly (Composed of:-		25	25	
				30	30	
21A		One 45-1-24 sling swivel				
23A		One 45-1-24 sling swivel plate (2)				
6C	45-1-6	Trigger		43	43	
6B	45-1-6	Trip		43	43	
32F	45-6-2	Washer, butt stock screw		58	58	
	B108828	Brush chamber cleaning M6	100	25	125	
	C4036	Brush cleaning cal.45 M5	200	100	300	
AOC139	15-18-98	Case accessory and spare parts M1918 Empty	100	10	110	
AOC132	ACC-132	Case 50 rnd, Cal.45 Mag w/shoulder strap	100	4	104	for use in tanks only
	15-18-102	Envelope 3" x 3 1/8" Empty	100	10	110	
	C7791	Gun sling M1923 "Webbing" (Slings Rifle Web)	100	25	125	
		Magazines 20 rnds Box type	1000	100	1100	
		Magazine, 50 rnds Drum type	2000	200	2200	
	C64151	Oiler (Can Oil)	100	10	110	
C64183	C64183	Rods cleaning S/M Gun	100	10	110	
	C64175	Thong Assembly complete	200	150	350	for use in tanks only
		Composed of one (A152700) Cord				
		One (A152701) Tip				
		One (A152701) Weight				

Chapter Twelve: The Return Spring Rod

The original 15,000 Thompson submachine guns manufactured by Colt's Patent Fire Arms Manufacturing Company in 1921/22 were Model of 1921. This was the model first ordered by the British military in 1940 before the order was changed to the Model of 1928 (p. 2). A Model of 1928 Thompson is but a modification of the original Model of 1921. The 1928 model was designed at the request of a good customer, the United States Marine Corps, which wanted the Thompson gun to have a slower rate of fire. Auto-Ordnance, always eager to please any customer, designed a heavier actuator (Table IV - B.E. 4008, Handles, cocking) that resulted in a slower rate of fire. During this same time period, the U.S. Navy took note of the Marines effective use of the Thompson submachine gun in the jungles of Nicaragua in 1926 and also began procurement of the Thompson albeit in small numbers. A Model of 1928 with the heavier actuator along with a new smaller diameter recoil spring and one piece buffer and pilot, horizontal forearm, sling and Cutts Compensator was marketed as the U.S. Navy model. Thompsons were taken from inventory and the 1921 markings were changed with the stamping of the number 8 over the number 1. This over stamping appears to many as the letter B, but it signifies a Model of 1928 Thompson. It is common to find the words "U.S. Navy" added to many Model of 1928 Thompson sold in the civilian market (usually to law enforcement organizations).

When Russell Maguire obtained control of the Auto-Ordnance Corporation in July 1939 the Model of 1928 was chosen for the new production. Aside from a heavy actuator, the 1928 model required a new buffer pilot, the part named by the British military as the Return Spring Rod (Table IV - British part B.E. 4018, Table V – B.E. 4019).[355] The USA Ordnance scale referred to this part as Pilot, buffer, part no. 17A (Table VII). The original smaller diameter Return Spring Rod (buffer pilot) for the Colt's and the very early Savage guns was manufactured without a hole at the long end of the rod. The absence of this hole made the removal and insertion of the rod difficult and often times caused the recoil spring to kink during installation.

from the Troy Scott collection, USA

An original and unmodified Return Spring Rod or buffer pilot from an early Savage Thompson in the 18,000 serial number range. Note there is no hole in the rod and the "S" marking is located on the side of the flange. The manufacturer marking is commonly found on the flat side of the flange. Also note the bevel at the end of the rod; another indication this is an early Return Spring Rod.

A solution was simple enough. Drill a small hole in the rod. And that is exactly what the British military did. Shown on the following page is D.D. (E) 2887 – "Instructions to Guide Modification to Return Spring Rod. Thompson, 45-IN. Machine Carbine," dated June 14, 1941. These instructions show unit armourers where and what size hole is to be drilled and then provide further instructions on assembly after the modification is performed.

---

[355] See pages 127 & 130, respectively. Additional documentation needed to determine which of these numbers is incorrect.

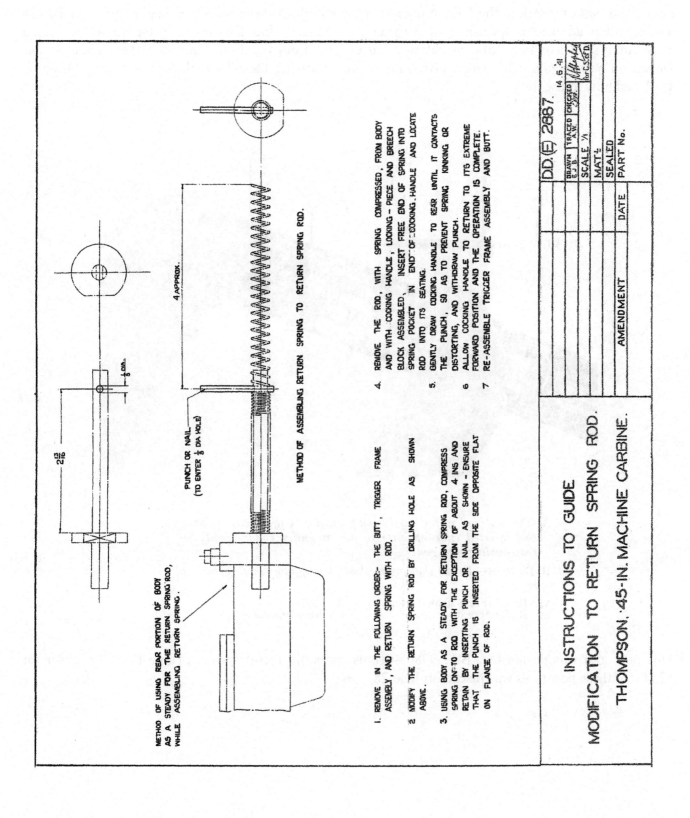

METHOD OF USING REAR PORTION OF BODY
AS A STEADY FOR THE RETURN SPRING ROD,
WHILE ASSEMBLING RETURN SPRING.

⅛ DIA.

2¹³⁄₁₆

PUNCH OR NAIL
(TO ENTER ⅛ DIA HOLE)

4 APPROX.

METHOD OF ASSEMBLING RETURN SPRING TO RETURN SPRING ROD.

1. REMOVE IN THE FOLLOWING ORDER:- THE BUTT, TRIGGER FRAME ASSEMBLY, AND RETURN SPRING WITH ROD.

2. MODIFY THE RETURN SPRING ROD BY DRILLING HOLE AS SHOWN ABOVE.

3. USING BODY AS A STEADY FOR RETURN SPRING ROD, COMPRESS SPRING ON-TO ROD WITH THE EXCEPTION OF ABOUT 4 INS AND RETAIN BY INSERTING PUNCH OR NAIL AS SHOWN - ENSURE THAT THE PUNCH IS INSERTED FROM THE SIDE OPPOSITE FLAT ON FLANGE OF ROD.

4. REMOVE THE ROD, WITH SPRING COMPRESSED, FROM BODY AND WITH COCKING HANDLE, LOCKING - PIECE AND BREECH BLOCK ASSEMBLED, INSERT FREE END OF SPRING INTO SPRING POCKET IN END OF COCKING HANDLE AND LOCATE ROD INTO ITS SEATING.

5. GENTLY DRAW COCKING HANDLE TO REAR UNTIL IT CONTACTS THE PUNCH, SO AS TO PREVENT SPRING KINKING OR DISTORTING, AND WITHDRAW PUNCH.

6. ALLOW COCKING HANDLE TO RETURN TO ITS EXTREME FORWARD POSITION AND THE OPERATION IS COMPLETE.

7. RE-ASSEMBLE TRIGGER FRAME ASSEMBLY AND BUTT.

INSTRUCTIONS TO GUIDE
MODIFICATION TO RETURN SPRING ROD.
THOMPSON .45-IN. MACHINE CARBINE.

DD.(E) 2887.

14 6 41

DRAWN E.J.B	TRACED A.W.	CHECKED
SCALE ½		
MAT⁵		
SEALED		
PART No.		

for C.S.&F D.

AMENDMENT	DATE

Inserting a nail or punch in the hole to compress the recoil spring was just the beginning. The British military then adopted a specific tool dedicated to compressing the recoil spring to assist during disassembly and assembly. Shown below is an excerpt from the 1942 Gale & Polden manual, *The Thompson Submachine Gun Mechanism Made Easy,* showing the new tool, Recoil Spring Stripping Tool, and how to use it.

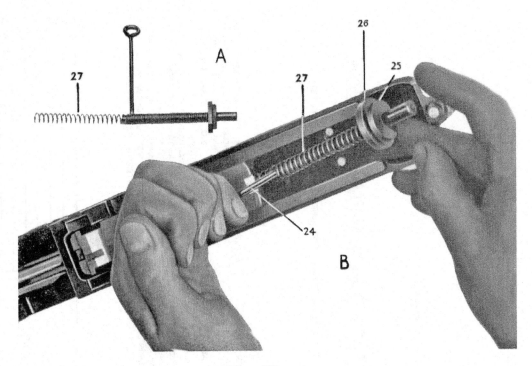

Plate IV

A TOP—*Recoil spring partly compressed on buffer rod, stripping tool inserted (side opposite to flat on buffer collar) ready for reassembling into gun.*

B BOTTOM—*Detail showing method of stripping recoil spring and buffer.*

24	Recoil spring stripping tool.	26	Buffer.
25	Buffer fibre disc.	27	Recoil spring.

This new tool was designated, B.E. 9986 - Tools assembly recoil spring, (Table IV). An order for 52,500 of these new tools was placed on June 28, 1941. [356]

---

[356] Order form for 52,500 B.E. 9986, Tools assembly recoil spring, signed by N.S. Oxford for the C.O.O. Weedon, dated June 28, 1941

Chapter Thirteen: Aerial Combat

Numerous instruction manuals and user handbooks about the operation and care of the Thompson gun have been produced over its long history. The number and types of manuals in many languages increased dramatically during World War II as the Thompson gun was adopted by allied forces. One of the more interesting and rarer manuals is reprinted in part, below. It is a British Admiralty Book of Reference and titled: B.R. 646, Instructions for Glider Target Range Using Thompson Guns, 1942. The manual describes a training course of fire using the Thompson gun to shoot at aerial targets. Aerial combat training normally involved a sleeve target towed by an aircraft and fired upon by a rifle caliber or larger weapon. When towed targets were not available, glider targets could be used as depicted in this training course using the Thompson gun as a sub-caliber substitute weapon. The manual compares the ballistics of the .45 caliber to the standard British .303 caliber and states, "The Thompson gun can be used to represent either a Lewis gun or, with its butt removed, a Hotchkiss." Safety in training and in real life aerial combat is stressed as it is very possible to shoot at adjacent ships or the masts and superstructure of the gunners own ship during training or a real life situation. Both box and drum magazines can be used in the training; the box magazine giving 2 seconds and the drum magazine 5 seconds of continuous firing. Note the reference to "Wren operators" on the course diagram; Wren is short for Women's Royal Naval Service. These were female civilians in uniform used to free up men for more active service. They did not go to sea, although some managed small boats in harbours. As revealed in Chapter Four, the Thompson gun was intended for issue to unarmed supply ships so it would be readily available for this type of training.

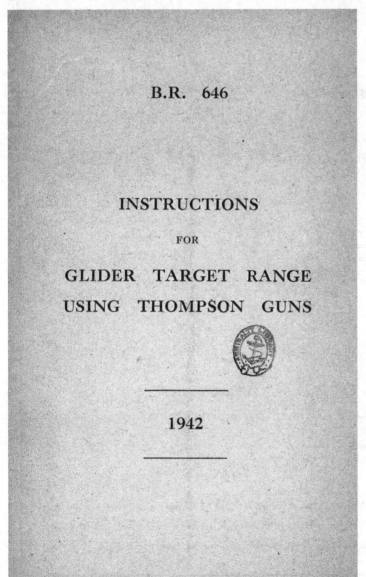

LEFT: The cover of B.R. 646 (from the Small Arms Review Reference Library, USA)

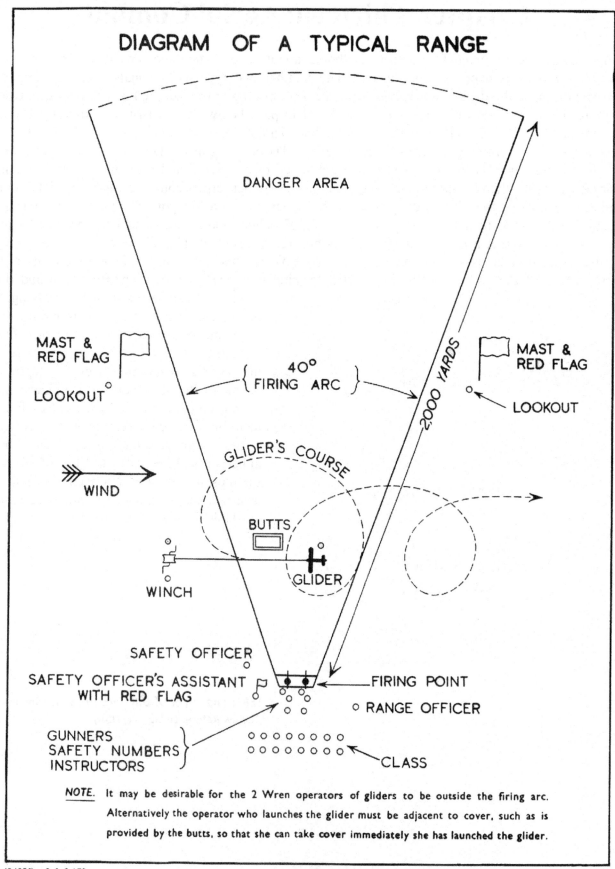

Diagram of a typical aerial range as depicted in B.R. 646

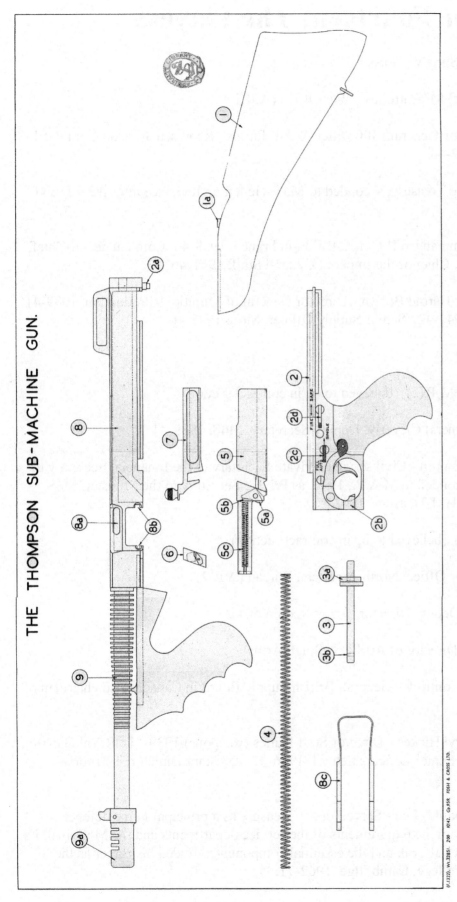

THE THOMPSON SUB-MACHINE GUN.

LEFT: Principal parts of the Thompson submachine gun as described in Admiralty B.R. 646:

1 Butt
1a Butt catch
2 Trigger Group
2a Trigger Group Catch
2b Magazine Catch
3 Return Spring Buffer Rod
3a Buffer washer
3b Hole for punch
4 Return spring
5 Bolt assembly, including extractor
5a Hammer
5b Firing Pin
5c Firing Pin Spring
6 "H" piece
7 Cocking knob and piece
8 Receiver
8a Ejector plate
8b Horizontal grooves for drum magazine
8c Breech lubricator pads and holder
9 Barrel
9a Compensator

Chapter Fourteen: The Players

1. W.M. Allen – Ministry of Supply (MoS)

2. Lt. Colonel (later Brigadier) M. Antrobus - War Office (A.R.1)

3. (Sir) Clive Baillieu, Director-General, BPC, after Arthur Purvis. Representative on Combined Raw Materials Board, 1942-43.

4. A.F. Dobbie-Bateman - The Treasury, seconded to MoS. He left civil service after the war and became a clergyman

5. General A.F. Brooke - Commanded II Corps, B.E.F. in France, 1939-40. Commander-in-Chief, UK Home Forces 1940-41. Chief of the Imperial General Staff, 1941-46

6. Engineer Vice-Admiral Sir Harold Brown - Director General of Munitions Production, 1939-41, later Controller-General 1941-42. Senior Supply Officer, MoS, 1942-46

7. R. C. Bryant - MoS, S.S.9

8. R. (Robert) Burns – MoS, M.P.(c) (believed to be in contract section)

9. O.S. (later Sir Osmund Somers) Cleverly, Deputy Secretary, MoS, 1939-41

10. Edmund Gerald (E.G.) Compton - Civil servant. Private Secretary to the Financial Secretary to the Treasury, 1934-36. Seconded to M.A.P., 1940, as Private Secretary to the Minister. MoS 1941. Assistant Secretary, HM Treasury, 1942.

11. R. Cullen – MoS, M.P. (c) (believed to be in contract section)

12. Colonel L.F.S Dawes - War Office. North American Bureau (A.R.2)

13. Brigadier D.R.D. Fisher - Deputy Director, Army Requirements

14. F.M.S. Gibson - Assistant Director of Artillery (Small Arms)

15. Colonel J.H.M. Greenly - Controller-General, British Supply Board in Canada, also chairman of Babcock & Wilcox

16. Maj. General Lancelot Daryl Hickes - Director Staff Duties (weapons) 1939-41. Royal Garrison Artillery 1904; Instructor, Senior Officers School, 1936-37; Assistant Director, Territorial Army, 1938;

17. F. G. (later Sir Frank Godbould) Lee - Served in the Treasury as a principal in the defence material division dealing with the requirements of the service departments and the MoS in all its aspects, including raw materials, oil, and the essential components. Ended his career as the Master of Corpus Christi College, Cambridge, 1962-71.

18. Lt. Colonel Lawes - War Office. Q.M.G. House (this may be Major Laws)

19. W.E. Leigh - Purchasing Agent for Munitions, BPC

20. Maj.-General A.E. Macrae - MoS Representative at British Supply Board, Ottawa. 1939-41. Chief Superintendent of Design, Woolwich, 1937–39; Military Technical Adviser to Department of Munitions and Supply, Ottawa, Canada, 1941–45

21. Lt. General Sir Gordon (Nevil) Macready - Assistant Chief of the Imperial General Staff (A.C.I.G.S.)

22. A.J. Manson - MoS, M.P. (c) (believed to be in contract section)

23. Jean Monnet – A French political economist and diplomat. Sent to London in December 1939 to organize the British and French war industries; later became the head of the Anglo-French Coordinating Commission. After the war, Monnet was one of the founding fathers of the European Union.

24. E.G. Penman – MoS, M.P.(f) (believed to be in finance section)

25. Arthur Blakie Purvis - Director-General, British Purchasing Commission (BPC), and later Chairman, Anglo-French Purchasing Board. Killed in an air crash, Aug.1941

26. Colonel E.M. Ransford - Director of Small Arms and Ammunition, British Purchasing Commission in Washington. Joint Chairman, Small Arms & Small Arms Ammunition Technical Committee (UK/Canada). Deputy Chairman, UK & Canada Joint Inspection Board (1944)

27. Sir Arthur Robinson - MoS, London. Permanent Secretary, later Deputy Chairman, Supply Board, later became a director of Babcock & Wilcox

28. R.J. (later Sir Robert) Sinclair- War Office. Director General of Army Requirements 1939-42. Also Chairman of Imperial Tobacco.

29. Lt. General Sir Maurice G. Taylor - Senior Military Advisor to the Minister of Supply, 1939-41. Formerly Deputy Master-General of the Ordnance.

30. G.W. (later Sir George) Turner – MoS, Principal Assistant Secretary (Production), 1939. Under-Secretary (General) 1941. Second Secretary, Supply (1942).

31. General Sir Walter Venning - Director General, British Supply Mission, Washington, 1942-46. Previously Quartermaster-General To The Forces.

32. Lord Weir - Industrialist, director of G & J Weir Pumps. Director of Explosives at the MoS, 1939-41. Briefly chairman of the Tank Board. Director of I.C.I., International Nickel, and numerous other companies.

33. Lt. Colonel H.J. Wright – A.D.W.S. at W.S.14 section

Chapter Fifteen: Acronyms and Abbreviations

Abbreviation	Explanation
A.D.S.A.	Assistant Director [of Artillery] Small Arms – see A.D.A.(S.A.), below
A.D.W.S.	(exact definition unknown)
A.F.V.	Armoured Fighting Vehicles
A.S.P.	Army Supply Program [U.S.]
'A' Programme	Program to form fifty-five divisions with British-produced equipment
'B' Programme	Program to provide Britain w/10 divisions of US Pattern military equipment
B.A.D.	British Admiralty Delegation [Washington]
B.A.S.	British Army Staff [Washington]
B.A.T.M.	British Admiralty Technical Mission [Ottawa]
B.E.F.	British Expeditionary Force. Refers to the force sent to France in 1939
B.P.C.	British Purchasing Commission (Washington)
B.S.B.	British Supply Board (Ottawa)
B.S.M.	British Supply Mission (Washington)
C.G.M.P.	Controller General of Munitions Production
C.I.A.	Chief Inspector, Armaments
C.I.S.A.	Chief Inspector, Small Arms
C.S.A.D.	Chief Superintendent, Armament Design
C.S.A.R.	Chief Superintendent, Armament Research
C.S.D.	Chief Superintendent, Design
D.A., D. of A.	Director of Artillery [responsible for design of small-arms]
A.D.A. (S.A.) (A3)	Assistant Director of Artillery (Small Arms) also abbreviated to A.D.S.A.
D.A. (S.A.)	Director of Artillery (Small Arms)
D.G. of A.	Director General of Artillery (upgraded to a Directorate during war)
D.A.D.O.S.	Deputy Assistant Director Ordnance Stores
D.A.F.V.	Director of Armoured Fighting Vehicles
D.A.S.C.	Defense Aid Supply Committee [U.S.]
D.D.G.P.	Deputy Director General of Production
D.D.G.O.F.	Deputy Director General Ordnance Factories
D.D.O.S.	Deputy Director Ordnance Stores
D.G.	Director General
D.G.A.R.	Director General of Army Requirements
D.G.M.P.	Director General of Munitions Production
D.G.W.P.	Director-General, Weapons Production
D. Inf	Director of Infantry
D.M.S.	Department of Munitions and Supply [Canadian]
D.S.D.(w)	Director Staff Duties (weapons)
E.R.C.	Exchange Requirements Committee of the Treasury, which authorizes the expenditure of dollars from the reserves.
I.G.A.	Inspector General, Armaments
I.R.A.	Irish Republican Army
I.S.A.A.	Inspector/Inspectorate Small Arms Ammunition

I.T.P.	Instructions To Proceed. Usually written, sometimes verbal. Allows the contractor to start work without waiting for a formal contract to be signed, or a contract price to be fixed.
I.W.O.	Initial War Orders. This is a misleading title; it may not be (probably is not) the initial order for this item. Later documents titled: Immediate War Orders. The plural word "Orders" is sometimes used in the singular.
M.A.C.	Munitions Assignments Committee
M.A.P.	Ministry of Aircraft Production
M.P.C.	Munitions Production Central
M.O.S. or MoS	Ministry of Supply
O.B.	Ordnance Board
O.C.	Ordnance Committee (became O.B. In 1939)
P.A.S.(P)	Principal Assistant Secretary (Production)
PA.S.(PR)	Principal Assistant Secretary (Priority)
P.& E.E.(P)	Proof & Experimental Establishment (Pendine)
R.S.A.F.	Royal Small Arms Factory [Enfield Lock]
S.A.I.D.	Small Arms Inspection Department [Enfield Lock]
S.A.S.	Small Arms School [Hythe - later moved to Bisley]
S.A.E.E.	Small Arms Experimental Establishment [initially co-located with S.A.S., moved in 1940 to Pendine Sands]
S. of D.	Superintendent of Design [Enfield Lock]
S.R.S.A.F	Superintendent, Royal Small Arms Factory
Schmeisser	MP28 copy which eventually became the Lanchester carbine
Stage One	Financial arrangements for providing aid to Britain up to the defeat Germany
Stage Two	Modified financial arrangements for providing aid to Britain between end of the German war and defeat of Japan, envisaged as lasting several years.
Victory Programme	Anglo-American production program of requirements for victory, produced late 1941, early 1942
W.O.	War Office
Z-Month	mobilization date, reckoned as Sept. 1939. Often referred to in documents in terms of Z+24, etc.

Chapter Sixteen:
The Tommy Gun in Great Britain Today

Private ownership of fully automatic weapons in the United Kingdom by ordinary citizens is just about non-existent. However, an original Thompson submachine gun can be purchased and taken home without permit or government approval. Unfortunately, these readily available World War II original Thompson guns have to first be permanently deactivated by a recognized Proof House and so marked. A deactivation certificate is generated for each deactivated weapon. Prior to October 1995, the deactivation process in Great Britain allowed for moving parts inside the receiver. These are referred to as "old spec" weapons. The deactivation process in place since October 1995 mandates the receiver or action must be welded shut, thus the bolt cannot be cocked or the weapon dry fired. These are referred to as "new spec" weapons. The "old spec" weapons are normally in much more demand and usually more expensive.

A deactivation certificate does not technically need to accompany a deactivated firearm in Great Britain. Nonetheless, it is a good practice to keep the paperwork and the deactivated firearm together in case any questions of legality arise. Shown below is a partial copy of a deactivation certificate for an American Thompson submachine gun.

Number DA 16585 12249

Certificate of **De-Activation**

PROBIS CIVIBUS CANONES PROBENTUR

The London Proof House hereby certifies that the work has been carried out on the firearm described below in a manner approved by the Secretary of State under Section 8 of the Firearms (Amendment) Act 1988 for the rendering it incapable of discharging any shot, bullet or other missile.

No firearm certificate is required to possess this gun

Type and Make: Machine Gun, THOMPSON

Calibre/Chamber Length: .45"ACP Barrel Length: 10.50"

Number: 86612 Country of Origin: U.S.A.

146

There has always been a certain mystic about the Thompson gun in the United States. That same fervor found its way to Great Britain in 1940 and remains there today. Shown below is an old spec deactivated Savage Thompson, serial number S-86612, sent to Great Britain during cash-and-carry that survived the war and later escaped (complete) destruction when no longer needed for military service. Deactivated weapon collections are commonplace in Great Britain. Examples of most World War II weapons are usually easy to find and acquire.

from the James West collection, Great Britain

The left and right side receiver markings of Savage manufactured Thompson submachine gun, serial number S-86612. This Thompson gun is an "old spec" deactivation and legal for civilian ownership in Great Britain. A close-up picture of the left side receiver markings for S-86612 can be found in Chapter Two. Note the Bridgeport, Connecticut address and location of the patent number markings on the right side – see Chapter Ten. This is a very early Bridgeport marked Savage Thompson. The actuator or cocking knob is knurled but the fire control levers lack this feature. The ejector is the flat early milled type. The magazine catch has a hole toward the end, indicative of the late style catch.

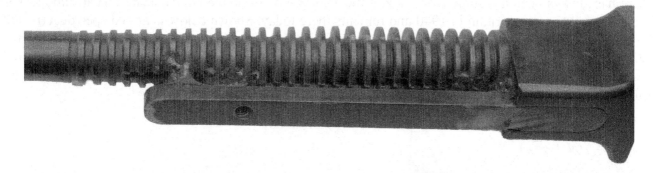

from the James West collection, Great Britain

The barrel of S-86612 has been destroyed and permanently affixed to the receiver. Note the slot cut underneath the grip mount and how the grip mount has been welded to the receiver and barrel. The deactivation process is performed with great care so the weapon will be permanently disabled, but allows the horizontal wood fore grip to hide most of the handiwork. This makes for a great display Thompson gun. Note the square S marking on the left side of the grip mount (see arrow and close-up picture inset) in the second picture from the top. This was the mark of Stevens Arms Company, Chicopee Falls, Massachusetts, a subcontractor that manufactured numerous Thompson parts.

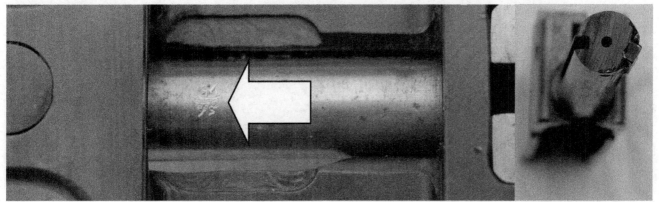

from the James West collection, Great Britain

The front end of the bolt is deactivated and marked (see arrow) by the Proof House. While the front of the bolt is sheared off at a 45-degree angle effectively destroying the bolt, the extractor can still be affixed to the bolt body for display purposes. The firing pin & spring, hammer and hammer pin were removed from the bolt and discarded.

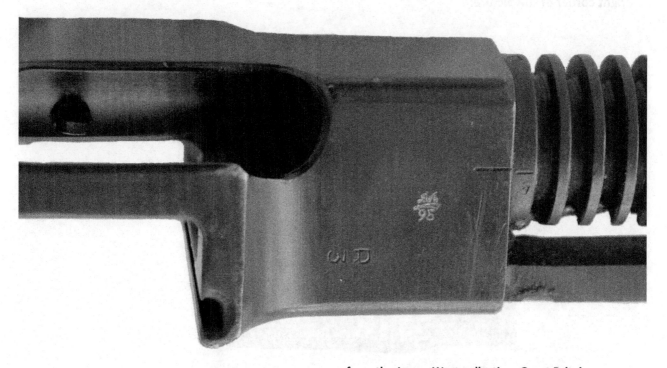

from the James West collection, Great Britain

The Proof House marking on the receiver nose identifies the Poof House and year of deactivation (1995). These marks must not be removed or altered.

The deactivation process can differ from gun to gun. The deactivated former IRA Thompson gun featured in Chapter Ten shows much more "work."

from the Dermot Foley collection, Great Britain

Arrow on bottom left: note how a portion of the receiver rails on the bottom of the receiver has been removed in the deactivation process of this Thompson gun (compared to S-86612 as pictured earlier in this chapter). Arrow on right: note the Proof House markings in the lower right corner of the picture.

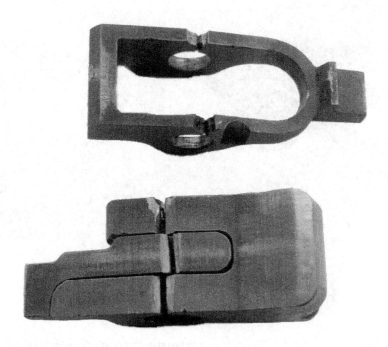

from the Dermot Foley collection, Great Britain

The deactivation process for the former IRA Thompson included the internal parts in the frame. Nearly every part of this historical Thompson gun was rendered inoperable.

150

The annual War and Peace Show in Kent, England, now known officially as the War and Peace Revival Show, is a great place to find a deactivated Thompson gun. This show has a long history in Great Britain. The 31st annual show, in conjunction with the Military Vehicle Preservation Society, was held on July 17-21, 2013. Shown below are pictures of deactivated Thompson guns readily available for purchase. The price for a "new spec" Thompson is approximately £450 or $725.

Photograph by Robert Segel, Senior Editor, Small Arms Review
There is no shortage of deactivated Thompson guns at the War and Peace Show each year.

Photograph by Robert Segel, Senior Editor, Small Arms Review
A M3A1 "Grease Gun" at the top, Model of 1928A1 Thompsons below and M1A1
Thompsons on the other side – a Thompson enthusiasts dream!

The 2014 War and Peace Show also featured numerous deactivated Tommy guns for sale. Shown to the left is a crate of M1/M1A1 Thompson guns awaiting new homes. Careful inspection of the picture will review milled and stamped sling swivels on the butt stocks and fore grips.

Photograph by Robert Segel, Senior Editor, Small Arms Review

153

Epilogue

This story is about how one small order of 750 Thompson submachine guns grew to over a half-million and became a part of British history. In the United States of America, the Thompson gun was initially held in very low esteem because of how it was used by the criminal element in the 1920s and 30s. The reputation in Great Britain was quite similar because of how the Thompson gun was used by the Irish Republican Army. However, all the features that initially made General Thompson's dream of a hand-held automatic weapon militarily unacceptable caused it to become one of the most sought after weapons during World War II.

Despite claims by many writers and experts over the last 90 years, General John Taliaferro Thompson was not the inventor of the Thompson submachine gun. General Thompson was the developer. He formed Auto-Ordnance Corporation, secured the necessary financing, and hired the brilliant engineers (Theodore H. Eickoff and Oscar V. Payne) who ultimately invented the Thompson gun. He also provided the necessary oversight, encouragement and military expertise to insure the successful invention of the first weapon named - submachine gun. General Thompson passed away on June 21, 1940. He never witnessed the complete change in reputation of this weapon named after him; a weapon so vilified *TIME* magazine described it as "...the deadliest weapon, pound for pound, ever devised by man..." [357] In one of General Thompson's last writings, he recounted his worries of how the Thompson gun had been used by evil men who were not "On the Side of Law & Order." His wish was quite simple, "May the deadly T.S.M.G. always "speak for" God & Country." [358] And so it did with so many British soldiers, commandos, sailors, airmen and Home Guard volunteers.

LEFT: General John Taliaferro Thompson, Brigadier General, U.S. Army (Retired), as pictured in his official biography, dated 1939.

---

[357] "Chopper," *Time,* June 26, 1939, 67
[358] William J. Helmer, *The Gun That Made The Twenties Roar* (Canada: Macmillan, 1969) 179 - a 1939 letter from General Thompson to Theodore H. Eickoff, former Chief Engineer at AOC

One last word…

The thought of young boys playing army or cops & robbers in the middle of a world war would seem incredulous to many in this politically correct world of today. Nonetheless, it happened routinely in the world of the greatest generation. That generation of men and women who stopped the lunatics from Germany, Italy and Japan from enslaving the world. The American gangster gun fought on all fronts during the Great War. Those of us that study this weapon become quickly aware everyone who has ever used it in battle or simply carried it on the job never forget the time they spent with this now iconic firearm. The Thompson gun was a news photographers dream; an easy sell to any editor. It should be of no surprise the children raised during the war that were too young to fight but not die have fond memories of this weapon too. That big drum magazine was a sign of strength, of good…of winning. Without a doubt, the young boys shown below instinctively knew this weapon called the Thompson, this Tommy gun, would always protect them from evil.

An ACME Newspicture, New York Bureau, dated February 7, 1943, captioned, "DIS IS A HOLDUP, BUD." The story reads, "London, England – A jeep driver for the U.S. Army Fire Guard, is the victim of a "HOLDUP", engineered by two young Londoners with a toy tommy gun. The "HOLDUP" was staged as Cpl. Milliman took part in "Wet Drill" competitions at the National Fire Service Headquarters in London. PASSED BY CENSORS"

About the author

Tom Davis, Jr. was born and raised as a dependent in the US Air Force so all of his early years were spent with his family traveling from one air base to another. His father was a pilot on duty and an amateur gunsmith at home. He was also a life member of the National Rifle Association. This provided Tom with an early introduction to firearms and monthly access to *The American Rifleman* magazine. Tom has been a Thompson enthusiast since his childhood, watching Robert Stack on *The Untouchables* and Vic Morrow on *Combat!*

Tom completed his undergraduate studies at Middle Tennessee State University in Murfreesboro, Tennessee and graduated with a Bachelor of Science in Criminal Justice Administration. He then attended the Nashville School of Law and graduated with a Doctor of Jurisprudence. He is licensed to practice law in Tennessee.

Tom's professional life involved working for several local law enforcement organizations, practicing law for a few years, and teaching Business Law at his college alma mater. Seeking a return to law enforcement Tom became an Inspector in 1986 at the U.S. Treasury Department, Internal Revenue Service, Office of Regional Inspector, an organization that specialized in internal crimes and the protection of the tax administration system in the United States. In 1999, Tom's organization was taken out of the IRS and became the Treasury Inspector General for Tax Administration. Tom retired in 2010 as an Assistant Special Agent in Charge in Cincinnati, Ohio.

While Tennessee is considered home, Tom has spent many years in Texas and now lives in Northern Kentucky. Tom is an avid Skeet competitor, something that often takes him away from the Thompson community. Tom and his lovely wife, Janet, have one wonderful child, Thomas, and a very loveable Lakeland terrier named Tango.

CPSIA information can be obtained
at www.ICGtesting.com
Printed in the USA
LVOW03s1617170316

479628LV00005B/14/P